PALIN
NATION

PALIN
NATION

CHANGING AMERICA
FROM OUTSIDE THE BELTWAY

Dr. David L. Goetsch
Dr. Archie P. Jones

WHITE HALL PRESS
WHITE HALL, WV

Palin Nation
Changing America from Outside the Beltway

© 2009 by David L. Goetsch and Archie P. Jones

Published by **White Hall Press**
44 Mountain Park Drive
White Hall, WV 26554

Printed in the United States of America.

Cover by LovelaceDesign

ISBN13: 978-1-6623-278-8

CONTENTS

INTRODUCTION

REAL CHANGE FOR A CHANGE

Sarah Palin is the most refreshing personality to emerge onto the national political scene since Ronald Reagan. She is bright, attractive, articulate, experienced, and quintessentially American. No political candidate since Ronald Reagan has been able to generate more excitement at both ends of the political spectrum than Sarah Palin. The left abhors her and the right adores her.

In fact, the reaction of the left to Sarah Palin is so visceral that it borders on hate. It is no exaggeration to say that she is the personification of everything the left considers objectionable about conservatives, America, and life in general. Sarah Palin is the left's worst nightmare: a conservative, Christian, anti-abortion, pro-gun, pro-family woman who, in spite of their best efforts to destroy her, remains a viable presidential candidate with broad popular appeal. The left is so frightened by the prospect of this conservative, Christian, moose-hunting hockey mom occupying the Oval Office that their reaction to her is often completely irrational. It is a reaction informed more by fear and paranoia than logic or reason.

This book began as an attempt to answer one simple but profound question: *What will Sarah Palin have to do to win the White House in 2012?* In answering this question however, we quickly started to realize that Sarah Palin is much more than a potential candidate for president. Sarah has shown America what can be accomplished with the proper focus. Her example is a needed lesson for every person in every field—whether it's politics, business, industry, government, education, or the military. Hers is a story of Horatio Alger proportions. It is one that people hoping to create a better life for themselves and others would do well to emulate. Regardless of the outcome of the presidential election of 2012, grassroots Americans must begin to rebuild the country from *outside* the beltway by emulating Sarah Palin's example of applying the traditional values of diligence, self-reliance, responsibility, accountability, perseverance, and hard work.

When she appeared on the national political stage, seemingly out of nowhere, Sarah Palin quickly became the target of choice for venomous attacks from the left. Almost overnight, she was reduced to a poster child for everything that separates the right from the left in American culture. It's as if the left needed one individual who could serve as the focal point for everything they view as being wrong with the world. Hate must have an object and for the left they couldn't have chosen a better focal point than Sarah Palin, because she so completely exemplifies everything to which they are opposed.

Of the left's various constituent groups, feminists seem to have the most vitriolic reaction to Sarah Palin. "The reaction to Palin revealed a deep and intense cultural paranoia on the left: an inclination to see retrograde reaction around every corner, and to respond to it with vile anger. A confident, happy, and politically effective woman who was also a social conservative was evidently too much to bear. The response of liberal feminists was in this respect particularly telling, and especially unpleasant."[1]

Noted feminist, Gloria Steinem, had this to say about Sarah Palin: "Having someone who looks like you and behaves like them, who looks like a friend but behaves like an adversary, is worse than having no one."[2] "[Palin] does not fit the feminist stereotype. She's just a high-achieving mom who comes from the common people. Consider every major controversial issue in American politics and culture right now and somehow, they touch her personally. Start with the most obvious: abortion."[3] Essentially, what feminists dislike about Sarah Palin is that she is a woman who rejects their beliefs, disdains their false claims of being victims, has a traditional family she loves, and, to add insult to injury, has tremendous popular appeal. Feminists harbor a deep-seated phobia that a woman who does not share their left-leaning outlook on life might actually become America's first female president.

Running a close second behind feminists in their angry paranoia about Sarah Palin are the intellectual elites—the condescending few who believe that only they are equipped to govern the many. Intellectual elites believe that an Ivy-League credential—or at least a degree from one of America's more prominent liberal universities—is a necessary prerequisite to service in high office. A degree from a state college or university is simply not acceptable in their eyes.

Sarah Palin is a bright, articulate, charismatic, well-educated individual who got that way without the help of

Harvard, Yale, Princeton, Columbia, or any other so-called top-tier institution. She earned a baccalaureate degree in journalism with a minor in political science from the University of Idaho. Her athletic background, love of hunting, and folksy charm endear her to the people that the intellectual elite arrogantly look down their noses at: everyday Americans—the ones who do America's work and fight America's wars.

Make no mistake, feminists and intellectual elitists are not especially threatened by Sarah Palin as an individual but by the "sleeping giant" that she represents. The greatest fear of the political left is that everyday Americans will once again be awakened by a president who respects them and shares their traditional American values—the type of thing that happened during the Reagan administration. They are right to be concerned. Just as Jimmy Carter's domestic and foreign policy blunders set the stage for a Ronald Reagan victory in 1980, Barack Obama's broken promises and socialistic policies are setting the stage for a Sarah Palin victory in 2012.

A Nobody from Nowhere

The things liberals dislike most about Sarah Palin are the same things that make her a viable presidential candidate. After four years of Barack Obama's broken promises, socialist economic policies, worldwide apology tours, naïve foreign policy, corrupt administrative practices, and anti-family values, the American public is going to be ready for a straight-talking, honest president who shares their values and deeply-held beliefs. They will be ready for a president who understands that America represents the world's last best hope for freedom and liberty, one who agrees with Alexis de Tocqueville that America is great because America is good.

William J. Bennett had this to say about America being the world's last best hope for freedom and liberty: "I believe America is still that hope, but I also believe that our conviction about American greatness and purpose is not as strong today. Newspaper columns and television reports are full of cynicism. Many express doubts about American motives on the world stage."[4] Ronald Reagan restored America's hope after the four-year malaise of the Carter administration. Reagan reminded all Americans that the "abiding sense of American greatness, of American purpose, of American exceptionalism has long characterized many of our leaders and tens of millions of the rest of us as well. We have long had hope."[5]

Like Reagan, Sarah Palin is the type of straight-talking, down-to-earth leader who can remind Americans of what is best about them and their country. She has the potential to be the type of leader with "an abiding sense of America's greatness, of American purpose, of American exceptionalism." This makes her not only a viable presidential candidate, but a potentially great motivator in the mold of Ronald Reagan.

The words of Senator John McCain when he introduced her as his vice-presidential running mate show why Sarah Palin is a viable candidate for our nation's highest office:

I have found the right partner to help me

stand up to those who value their privileges over their responsibilities, who put power over principle, and put their interests before your needs. I found someone with an outstanding reputation for standing up to special interests and entrenched bureaucracies; someone who has fought against corruption and the failed policies of the past; someone who's stopped government from wasting taxpayer's money.[6]

Sarah Palin was portrayed by detractors as a nobody from nowhere and by supporters as an overnight success. In truth, when John McCain introduced her as his running mate, Sarah Palin had been working toward that singular event for most of her forty-four years, and she was well-prepared for national office. "In her political life, Sarah Palin has displayed many of the traits that will define successful leaders of this century. Although far from perfect, she harbors a deep Christian faith and dogged determination to make government work for the people, rather than people for the government. Palin's style of leadership invites each of us, whatever our political bent to embrace challenge as opportunity and difficulty as hope."[7]

Rebuilding the Ruins

After four years of Jimmy Carter's disastrous performance in domestic affairs—in particular the economy, weakness in foreign affairs, and the Iran hostage debacle—Americans were looking for a strong leader who could restore their confidence, pride, and self-respect. President Carter set the stage for a conservative tidal wave that Ronald Reagan masterfully rode into the White House.

President Obama is now doing for Sarah Palin what Carter did for Reagan. By the time Barack Obama has subjected the American public to four years of broken promises, domestic ineptitude, foreign policy naiveté, environmental totalitarianism, and socialist economic policies, America will be ready for a strong leader who—like Reagan—can restore America's confidence, pride, and self-respect. That leader can be Sarah Palin if she and her advisors wisely use the time between now and the next presidential election and follow the example of Ronald Reagan.

Reagan spent the years leading up to his presidential campaign laying a solid foundation by studying the principles of politics and economics, building bridges to the American people, winning friends, and helping colleagues. During the campaign he presented himself as what he was: the antidote to Carter's weakness and a breath of fresh air when our country needed it most. Sarah Palin must do the same thing. She must use her time before the next presidential campaign to lay a solid foundation and motivate and encourage others to do likewise—at every level of government. During the campaign, she must differentiate herself from Barack Obama and force him to take full responsibility for trying to undermine the Constitution and convert America into a European-style socialist state. She can do this by effectively applying the following *big-ticket* strategies; strategies that could put her in the White House and give conservatives an opportunity to lead America back to greatness:

- Be Sarah Palin—refuse to be leashed, muzzled, or remolded by timid advisors

- Commit to restoring the sovereignty and integrity of the Constitution

- Reject socialism—commit to restoring capitalism, entrepreneurship, and the traditional work ethic

- Be forthright in pointing out the failings of secular humanism and unapologetic about America's Christian heritage

- Do not apologize to our allies or enemies—put America first in foreign policy and support our military

- Hold President Obama responsible for his broken promises and socialist policies

Each of these strategies is presented in detail in Chapters 1-6. In Chapter 7, we recommend several practical solutions to overcoming the major obstacles to a conservative revolution in 2012. Taken together the various recommendations and strategies presented in this book represent a comprehensive plan, the vision for which is the changing of America—from outside the beltway.

NOTES:

1. Yuval Levin, "The Meaning of Sarah Palin." Retrieved from https://www.commentarymagazine.com/viewarticle.cfm/the-meaning-of-sarah-palin-1467 on August 16, 2008.

2. Gloria Steinem. As quoted in "The meaning of Sarah Palin." Retrieved from https://www.commentarymagazine.com/viewarticle.cfm/the-meaning-of-sarah-palin-1467 on August 16, 2008.

3. Joe Hilley, *Sarah Palin: A New Kind of Leader* (Grand Rapids, MI: Zondervan, 2008), 12.

4. William J. Bennett, *America: The Last Best Hope* (Nashville, TN: Nelson Current, 2006), xiii.

5. *Ibid.*

6. John McCain as quoted in Joe Hilley, *Sarah Palin: A New Kind of Leader,* 23.

7. Hilley, 29.

One

Be Sarah Palin

"I was just your average hockey mom, and signed up for the PTA because I wanted to make my kid's public education better."

—Sarah Palin

It was one of the most memorable nights in the history of American politics. The setting was the Nutter Center at Wright State University in Dayton, Ohio. The arena was packed with loyal Republicans, and the air was thick with anticipation and suspense. Everyone in attendance knew that this was the night they would finally learn the name of John McCain's running mate. In the weeks leading up to that night, the press, media, and political pundits had stoked the rumor mill to a red-hot fury. All Americans—Republicans, Democrats, and Independents—were eager to learn the name of his selection.

Having played his cards close to his chest for months, McCain was in no hurry to reveal his secret. After all, the rampant speculation about his running mate actually helped him by forcing a blatantly pro-Obama press corps to cover the McCain campaign. McCain, not known for his dexterity at the podium, actually did a masterful job of playing the moment for all it was worth. When, at long last, he felt the stage was properly set for maximum effect,

John McCain finally said: "I am very pleased and very priv-ileged to introduce to you the next vice-president of the United States... Governor Sarah Palin of the great state of Alaska." His announcement set off a firestorm of interest that for a few brief moments in history eclipsed even the well-oiled, media-assisted public-relations juggernaut of Barack Obama. Sarah Palin was an instant sensation. She energized the right wing of the Republican Party, engaged the interest of the press and media, frightened the left, and fascinated the American public.

Unfortunately for the McCain campaign, the firestorm of excitement created by Sarah Palin soon dwindled into nothing more than a gentle breeze. Some blamed this turn of events on the vicious, hypocritical smear campaign launched against Sarah Palin by the left. While the media should not be excused for its blatant lack of journalistic ethics, it is important for conservatives to understand that the left—in spite of its best efforts—did not undermine Sarah Palin's effectiveness on the campaign trail. They did not have to. Timid advisors in the McCain campaign and Republican Party achieved that dubious goal for them.

The McCain campaign made many mistakes, but by far the biggest was listening to advisors who wanted to leash, muzzle, and remold Sarah Palin. In the campaign, the Republican Party's best and worst decisions both in-volved Sarah Palin. Its best decision was naming Sarah Palin as its vice-presidential candidate. Its worst decision was putting a leash and muzzle on Palin and trying to re-mold her into something she wasn't. Cautious advisors in the McCain camp failed to recognize the nature of Palin's

Ronald Reagan-like appeal to Americans. Consequently, rather than get out of the way and let Sarah be Sarah, they tried to remold her in an ill-advised attempt to appeal to selected voters who never would have voted for her in any case or under any circumstances.

Many times during his campaigns and presidency, similar advisors tried to put a leash and a muzzle on Ronald Reagan. For example, advisors tried repeatedly to convince Reagan to remove the line—"Mr. Gorbachev, tear down this wall"—from his famous Berlin speech. Reagan, who had an instinctive feel for an audience as well as a staunch dedication to sound principles, ignored the advice and the rest is history. People who advise presidential candidates spend too much time in Washington, DC and too little time in grassroots communities where everyday Americans live and work. Like Reagan, Sarah Palin has enormous appeal at the grassroots level. In order to make the most of that appeal, the Republican Party will need to get out of the way and let Sarah be Sarah.

Why Sarah Palin Appeals to Americans— Her "Ten Cs"

No politician since Ronald Reagan has appealed to grassroots Americans on such a personal level as Sarah Palin. There is good reason for her appeal. In her, Americans see not so much who they are, but who they would like to be. As only the most effective leaders can, Sarah Palin inspires people to believe in her by being a positive example of what they would like to be themselves. Of course, few people consistently live up to their highest ideals, and Sarah Palin is no exception. But rather than hurt her, this fact only reinforces her appeal to grassroots Americans who also struggle with not being perfect.

Sarah Palin exemplifies ten specific traits that many Americans admire, respect, and aspire to themselves. We call these traits the *Ten Cs of Sarah Palin,* and believe they are why she appeals to so many Americans. The last trait on the list is *credibility.* Presidential candidates must have credibility with the American public. Without credibility, a candidate has little or no chance of becoming president. The obvious question raised by this fact is: How does a candidate get credibility (not counting politically calculated and media-aided deceit)? Candidates earn credibility by exemplifying certain traits that are important to Americans. Sarah Palin not only exemplifies these critical traits, she personifies them:

- Clarity
- Character
- Candor
- Commitment
- Caring
- Courage
- Christianity
- Change agency
- Competitiveness
- Credibility

Sarah Palin exemplifies and personifies the first nine traits on this list, a fact that gives her credibility—the tenth trait—with the American public. If she refuses to allow her advisors to leash, muzzle, or remold her—in other words, if she insists that they let Sarah be Sarah—she will be the most viable presidential candidate since Ronald Reagan.

CLARITY

Clarity is essential to effective leadership. People want to know who their presidential candidates are, what they stand for, and where they propose to lead the country. Sarah Palin is a breath of fresh air in this regard. She is forthright, straightforward, and candid about who she is, what she stands for, and where she would like to lead America. This will be an important trait in the next election since Americans are already tiring of President Obama's deceitful rhetoric, broken promises, socialist economic policies, practiced equivocation, naïve foreign policy, and fascination with the delusion of international law.

Clarity of purpose was one of Ronald Reagan's most endearing traits. "Ronald Reagan was guided by a moral center that included a strong belief in God, firm commitment to individual liberty, and respect for free-market economics. From these core beliefs he developed a few, succinct governing objectives to which he held with almost obsessive devotion—reduce taxes, reduce the size of government, free small businesses from burdensome regulation, stand tough for the freedom and dignity of others."[1] Sarah Palin is as clear in her sense of purpose as Ronald Reagan was, and her purpose is strikingly similar to what his was.

Like Ronald Reagan, the first and most important point on the internal compass that guides Sarah Palin's

life is her faith in God. Also like Reagan, her core belief
in God is augmented by a deep and abiding commitment to such quintessentially American values as individual liberty, free-market economics, self-reliance,
self-sufficiency, individual responsibility, justice, and
accountability.

Sarah Palin is forthright concerning the specifics of
her beliefs. At various times and in various forums she has
consistently said that she:

- Opposes same-sex marriage

- Opposes embryonic stem cell research

- Opposes abortion, but also opposes punitive
  sanctions against women who have an abortion

- Supports the discussion of creationism in public schools, but not teaching it as part of formal
  classes

- Supports abstinence as part of sex education, but
  also supports the inclusion of birth control

- Supports Second Amendment rights to bear arms
  (including semi-automatic assault weapons)

- Supports gun-safety education

- Supports capital punishment for adults

- Supports oil and gas exploration wherever it
  makes sense and other approaches to energy
  independence

- Supports the military and pre-emptive strikes
  when necessary to eliminate imminent threats
  to America

Sarah Palin is clear on where she wants to lead our country. Her vision for America is that it will once again be the moral, economic, and military leader of the world; a nation of self-reliant, responsible citizens that take care of themselves, each other, and their communities; one that is charitable through private giving to the needy in other nations. On the basis of her record, one can deduce that, as president, Sarah Palin would commit to restoring America by reducing taxes, pursuing energy independence, committing to a strong national defense, getting government off the backs of businesses, reducing mindboggling government regulation, encouraging patriotism, standing up for the freedom and dignity of individual Americans, championing traditional values, fighting for justice, and setting an example of the entrepreneurial spirit and positive work ethic. If Sarah Palin is consistent with her record, clarity of vision will serve her well in the next presidential campaign, and as president.

CHARACTER

Nothing has a more powerful effect on a president's performance in office or legacy than his or her character. "Whether leading in business, education, politics, or family, character always trumps charisma. What we desperately need in our leaders today is strong character."[2] In spite of his brilliant coup in opening China to relations with America, President Nixon will always be remembered as the Watergate president. In spite of serving during a period of unprecedented economic growth, President Clinton will always be remembered for his dalliance with Monica Lewinsky. It is too early to know what President Obama's legacy might be, but one possibility is that he will be remembered as the president who turned the United States into a European-style socialist state drowning in debt.

In order for a president's legacy to be positive, he or she must be trusted by the American public. The trust of the American people is the most valuable asset a president can have. It is even more important than having a majority in Congress, a strong military, or a vibrant economy. In fact, one of the most fundamental principles of leadership is that people will not willingly follow a leader they do not trust. This principle explains, in part, the precipitous decline in President Obama's approval ratings during his first year in office. Many Americans came to believe that President Obama had broken numerous campaign promises and lied to them about such critical issues as healthcare, taxes, the role of lobbyists in his administration, the economic stimulus plan, post-racialism, and transparency in office, to name just a few. President Obama appears to have fallen into the same trap that has undermined the trustworthiness of many politicians: saying one thing and doing another.

Contrast President Obama's penchant for saying one thing but doing another with the consistency of Sarah Palin. Character is Sarah Palin's strong suit. She has shown herself to have an attitude toward life and politics that has been described as "a kind of moralistic anti-corruptionism, obsessed with honest dealing and powerfully allergic to excess and waste."[3] Sarah Palin is trustworthy because her actions—not perfectly but certainly consistently—match her words. Perhaps the best example of this phenomenon is her fifth child, Trig. Sarah Palin is decidedly pro-life, a fact well-known to both supporters and opponents. Before he was born, the Palins learned that Trig had Down syndrome. Many assumed that Sarah Palin would abort Trig, and some even encouraged her to do so. A sad fact is that 90 percent of mothers in the United States carrying a Down syndrome baby choose to abort it.

Even among her supporters there were those who said they would understand if she set aside her pro-life views because of what they called "special circumstances." Although she fully understood the challenges of raising a Down syndrome child, Sarah Palin never flinched in her commitment to bring baby Trig into the world. This was a refreshing change for Americans who were accustomed to hearing politicians say one thing but do another. For example, Americans heard Bill Clinton and Barack Obama campaign on the importance of public education in America only to see them put their own children in exclusive private schools once elected president. Like so many politicians, when faced with the practical consequences of their so-called convictions, Clinton and Obama balked and reversed course. Not so with Sarah Palin.

Another telling example of the character of Sarah Palin is her decision to forego a campaign for the United States Senate in 2004. She wanted the seat, felt she was right for it, and had strong backing if she decided to run. However, there was a stumbling block. Sarah Palin had always put the needs of her family ahead of her career. Adept at juggling the demands of career and family, the immovable object in her life remained family, not career. In the rare cases where one or the other had to give, family trumped career. The Senate race of 2004 was one of those cases.

She wanted the Senate position, felt sure she could win the race, and had the blessing of all members of her family; all, that is, except one. Her oldest son, Track, was not enthusiastic. If she won, the family would have to move to Washington, DC for much of the year. Track was in his senior year of high school and did not want to leave his friends. Like any young person in this situation, Track wanted to graduate with his long-time classmates, the friends he had grown up with. Sarah listened to her son's concerns and made her decision—no Senate run. True to her nature and character, Sarah Palin made a decision informed by her family-first beliefs rather than what she wanted personally.

Integrity is the key character trait for all leaders. It means living your life according to your professed values. It means living your life in such a way that your actions are consistent with your beliefs. People with integrity exemplify five bedrock characteristics:

Refusal to pretend. People with integrity are who they are and they refuse to pretend to be something else. After growing accustomed to politicians who are more concerned with image than substance—coifed, manicured, perfectly dressed mannequins who are really just empty suits—Americans found Sarah Palin's what-you-see-is-what-you-get attitude refreshing and appealing.

Application of an internal moral compass. Their values are so much a part of people with integrity that the individual and the values cannot be separated. All aspects of their daily lives are guided by their internal moral compass rather than by peer pressure, popularity polls, media coverage, or other political concerns. Americans found the fact that Sarah Palin lives her life according to a God-centered moral compass a welcome change of pace after what they have come to expect from politicians.

Consistency of actions and decisions. Their actions and decisions are predictable because people with integrity are consistent with their moral compass. Voters do not trust candidates or presidents whose decisions and actions are unpredictable. They like to know where people stand. Consequently, they do not like politicians whose views are constantly changing to match the results of opinion polls. Sarah Palin's life in politics has been a model of consistency. From the birth of her youngest child, Trig, to her decision to decline an opportunity to run for the United States Senate in 2004, her actions and decisions have been consistent with her beliefs.

Concerned with substance rather than image. Even the most carefully-crafted image will not withstand the microscopic scrutiny of today's 24-7-365 media coverage, especially if you are a conservative. Even liberal politicians who enjoy the assistance of the media find it difficult to maintain a false image for very long. An individual's substance or lack of it will eventually show through no matter how well-crafted his or her public image might be. Substance over image is one of the bricks in the foundation of Sarah Palin's appeal to the American public. It was not the new wardrobe the Republican Party purchased for her during the campaign that endeared her to Americans. She had already climbed the political ladder from city council to the governor's mansion without that wardrobe. Rather, it was her substance that made her such an appealing candidate; her what-you-see-is-what-you-get approach to politics, scripturally-based moral compass, consistency of beliefs and actions, and ability to relate to everyday Americans that voters found appealing.

Selflessness. One cannot be a self-centered, self-serving person and also be a person of integrity. An attitude that says "It's all about me" or "I'm looking out for number one" will not build trust. Over the long term, the best presidents are those who are good stewards of the ideals set forth in the Declaration of Independence and Constitution, those who leave office having made our country better morally, as well as more secure economically and militarily. To be good stewards, leaders must be willing to think first of others and put their needs ahead of their own. During the 2008 Presidential campaign, Americans were introduced to an individual who had spent her life doing precisely that—putting the needs of others ahead of her own. In Sarah Palin, they saw an individual who got involved in the PTA for the sole purpose of ensuring a better education for her children, did exhausting and dangerous work on fishing boats to help her husband support the family, ran for city council to help improve her community, ran for governor to eliminate corruption in her state's government, and declined an opportunity to run for the U.S. Senate so that her oldest son could graduate from high school with his classmates. In Sarah Palin, Americans saw a selfless leader who would put the good of the country ahead of her own ambitions, needs, and continuance in political office.

In an age when saying one thing but doing another is common practice, when making decisions on the basis of a me-first outlook is typical, and when glibly rationalizing differences between stated beliefs and actual practice is normal, Sarah Palin's consistency of character is both refreshing and encouraging. It sets her apart from most politicians in ways that will serve her well as a presidential candidate and as president.

CANDOR

The use of double-speak, obfuscation, prevarication, spin, and damage control has become just another day at the office in the world of politics. In fact, these things have been developed into an art form by politicians who lack candor. Americans have grown accustomed to vacuous politicians who use carefully-scripted but empty words to confuse rather than clarify and rationalize rather than explain. Further, they have grown weary of politicians who self-servingly clutter the airways with empty words rather than issuing a forthright apology when they make a mistake.

For example, President Obama caught a serious case of "foot-in-mouth disease" when in 2009 he called the Cambridge police "stupid" after a routine 911 call turned into an arrest of a Harvard professor who had not learned to mind his manners and cooperate. Rather than admit his error and simply apologize, Obama said he could have "calibrated" his words better—a case of blatant and arrogant prevarication. People with candor—people like Sarah

Palin—do not need to "calibrate" their words. Americans long for straight-talking leaders who use words to communicate not prevaricate.

Straight talking is why Ronald Reagan came to be known as the "great communicator." Though a gifted and eloquent speaker, he made a point of talking in a simple, frank manner that made his meaning clear. His goal was to ensure that listeners understood him, not to impress college professors or to appear to say one thing when he was actually saying something else. For example, there was little room for misinterpretation in his admonition, "Mr. Gorbachev, tear down this wall." The Soviet Union's leaders certainly understood when President Reagan called their country an "evil empire." Ronald Reagan said what he meant and meant what he said.

Contrast Reagan's straight talk with President Clinton's waffling during the Monica Lewinsky debacle. Contrast it with President Obama's no-lobbyists promise which he broke 17 times in his first two weeks in office (as well as breaking numerous other promises). Contrast it with what we are accustomed to hearing from most members of Congress and you will see why Sarah Palin's candor is a welcome relief to so many Americans. Sarah Palin says what she thinks in a straight-forward, frank manner reminiscent of Ronald Reagan. She uses words in an open, honest, plain-spoken manner to communicate, not prevaricate.

For an example of Sarah Palin's candor, examine her public statements. Almost without exception she is Reagan-like in her candor and effectiveness as a communicator. Consider the following excerpt from her acceptance speech at the Republican National Convention in St. Paul, Minnesota; the speech where she explained the difference between a pit bull and a hockey mom (lipstick):

> We are expected to govern with integrity, good will, clear convictions, and a servant's heart. I pledge to all Americans that I will carry myself in this spirit as vice president of the United States. This was the spirit that brought me to the governor's office, when I took on the old politics as usual in Juneau, when I stood up to the special interests, the lobbyists, big oil companies and the good-ol' boy's network.[4]

In this same speech, she put the left-leaning, pro-Obama media on notice when she said with perfect candor: "I'm not going to Washington to seek their (the media's) good opinion—I'm going to Washington to serve the people of this country."[5] Like Ronald Reagan, Sarah Palin uses words to connect with people, to communicate with them, and to conjure up images that help her listeners understand her. She uses words to clear away the fog that often surrounds complex issues, not to create more of it. After four years of broken promises by President Obama and the tiresome bromides of his minions in Congress, Sarah Palin's candor will serve her well in the next presidential election.

COMMITMENT

Effective leaders are steadfast, resolute, and willing to persevere to achieve their goals. In other words, they are committed. Commitment is one of Sarah Palin's strengths, a
fact she has demonstrated throughout her political career
and life. This is good news for Palin supporters because
commitment is essential to a presidential campaign and to
serving as president. People are reluctant to follow a leader who appears wishy-washy and noncommittal. Nor will
they follow a leader whose resolve they question. Effective
leaders must be steadfast in staying the course, especially
when doing so becomes difficult. Sarah Palin has shown
herself to be such a leader.

She entered political life because she wanted to make
Wasilla better for its citizens. A less committed leader
would have given up numerous times when faced with
the challenges Sarah Palin had to overcome in her campaigns and while serving as mayor and governor. When
she entered politics, Sarah Palin was an unknown, running
against entrenched opposition. Her opponent in the race
for Mayor of Wasilla was John Stein, a three-term incum-
bent. She had little money, no organization, only a cursory
knowledge of the issues, and, on top of all of this, a family
to raise. What she did have was a steadfast commitment
to make things better for her neighbors. Sarah Palin first
set her sights on becoming Mayor of Wasilla and then on
becoming Governor of Alaska. She won both campaigns
and served well in both offices.

Perhaps the best example of Sarah Palin's ability to
commit to a goal and persevere against the odds can be

found not in the political arena but on the basketball court. Sarah played basketball for Wasilla High School and although a fierce competitor, she was not the best player on the team. In fact, until she was a senior—much to her chagrin—she had to play on the junior varsity team. But Sarah did have a quality that set her apart from other players—perseverance. Commenting on this quality, her father said: "I look back on Sarah's perseverance and whatever she wanted to do, she put her nose to the grindstone, especially in sports. If she didn't have a certain ability, she worked and worked and worked until she had that ability."[6]

Sarah made the varsity team as a junior but spent most of her time warming the bench rather than playing. At the time she had more desire than ability. Upset about getting little court-time, she complained to her coach. He responded by suggesting she move down to the junior varsity and work on developing her skills. Embarrassed and angry about being sent down, Sarah nonetheless persevered. She worked with dedication and determination to sharpen her skills, and her hard work paid off. On the basis of her newly developed skills and leadership ability, Sarah was made the starting point guard and co-captain of the varsity team when the next season rolled around. During that season, she played with an intensity that earned her the now famous nickname "Sarah Barracuda."

If Sarah Palin runs for president in the next election, it is likely that she will once again be fighting against the odds. But if she continues her tradition of commitment and perseverance, Sarah Palin can beat those odds once again. In the next election, there will be plenty of voters accustomed to viewing Washington as the solution to their problems and who feel entitled to feed at the government trough. Those with socialist leanings will not like Sarah Palin's message of self-reliance and personal responsibility. Voters who have grown accustomed to riding in the government wagon will not like being asked to climb out and help others push. However, after four years of President Obama's European-style economic policies there will also be plenty of voters who understand that socialism is a one-way street to disaster. These Americans will be hungry for a candidate who will encourage entrepreneurship, a positive work ethic, self-reliance, and personal responsibility. If Sarah Palin remains committed to these values, she can become America's next president.

CARING

The most effective presidents have cared more about the country, the Constitution, and the American public than their own personal agendas and the perquisites of the office. The American people want to know that their president cares. This is one of the reasons Bill Clinton and Barack Obama were elected—they convinced Americans that they cared about them. It is also one of the reasons President Obama's approval ratings dropped so precipitously during his first year in office. As people learned more and more about the details of his economic and social policies, they began to question whether he really cared about the country, the Constitution, or them. Many began to believe he was bent on bankrupting America and its working citizens. The more they learned about his agenda, the less

Americans thought President Obama cared and, in turn, the more his approval rating dropped.

Sarah Palin, by way of contrast, has consistently showed that she cares about her family, community, state, and country. Her determination to give birth to baby Trig in spite of his Down syndrome was an act of caring at the most personal level. Her decision to forego running for the Senate in 2004 so that her oldest son, Track, could graduate with his long-time classmates was an act of caring. Although disappointed by her daughter Bristol's out-of-wedlock pregnancy, Sarah still provided her with emotional support and love. This act of kindness was yet another example of her capacity for caring.

One of Sarah Palin's first acts after being sworn in as Governor of Alaska was to get rid of the $2.7 million jet purchased in 2005 by her predecessor, Governor Murkowski. She thought the jet was an extravagant symbol of what was wrong with Alaska's state government, an insult to hardworking taxpayers—the very people she had entered politics to help. The fact that she attempted to sell the jet on eBay only endeared her to Alaskan citizens even more.

COURAGE

Presidential leadership requires courage, not necessarily physical courage but certainly moral courage. Although Sarah Palin has shown physical courage over the course of her life—such as helping out on her husband's fishing boat under sometimes dangerous conditions—it is her moral courage that will serve her well as a presidential candidate. It will also serve her well if she becomes president.

John McCain recognized Sarah's courage when he selected her as his running mate. In fact, it is one of the
reasons why he chose her. When introducing her as his
running mate, McCain said: "I found someone with an
outstanding reputation for standing up to special interests
and entrenched bureaucracies; someone who has fought
against corruption and the failed policies of the past;
someone who's stopped the government from wasting
taxpayer's money."[7] Fighting corruption, special interests,
and entrenched bureaucracies requires courage. Corrupt,
entrenched public officials and the special interest groups
that support them do not give up easily, and their favorite
tactic for fighting back is to destroy those who threaten
their kingdoms.

Because John McCain's selection of Sarah Palin as his
running mate drew the media's attention away from their
chosen son, Barack Obama, the left immediately retaliated.
They launched a smear campaign of unprecedented vicious-
ness designed to destroy Sarah Palin, her family, and her candidacy. Few people could have withstood the mean-spirited
onslaught directed at Sarah Palin, her husband, and her children, but she did. In fact, Sarah Palin not only withstood the
slander and libel from the left, she stood her ground valiantly
and fought back with determination, passion, and courage.
In the process, she won converts to the McCain campaign
that would not otherwise have voted for him.

Anyone can deliver good news or preach to the choir on
a given issue, but it takes courage to stand before a group
that you care about and that is important to your political
future and say "I am sorry but I cannot agree with you on

this issue." Many politicians faced with such a situation either back down from their position or try to placate their audience with platitudes and political spin. Sarah Palin is just the opposite. When she disagrees with a constituent group, she looks their representatives in the eye and respectfully tells them so.

Sarah Palin has faced this kind of situation numerous times in her political career and the outcome has usually been positive, because the constituent group in question admired her courage and candor. One such incident occurred during her 2006 campaign for governor. A group of trawlers and fish processors from Kodiak Island had an issue that was important to them. Sarah listened carefully to their concerns, but still could not support their position. She told them tactfully but firmly. Impressed that she did not duck the issue and with her willingness to listen, in spite of the fact that she disagreed with them, the group decided to support her campaign for governor in spite of their differences with her.

Perhaps the most courageous act of Sarah's political life occurred when Alaskans voted in 1998 to amend their state's constitution to preclude same-sex marriages. She supported the amendment. When she ran for governor, Sarah Palin was open and forthright about her opposition to same-sex marriages. But a problem arose. In response to the constitutional amendment, a number of state employees who were living together in homosexual relationships sued the state for denying benefits to their partners. When the lower court upheld the state's no-benefits policy, the plaintiffs appealed to Alaska's Supreme Court. The Supreme Court overturned the lower court and ordered that the same benefits provided to spouses in traditional marriages be given to the homosexual partners of state employees.[8]

The ruling by Alaska's Supreme Court resulted in a predictable uproar among supporters of the constitutional amendment and no-benefits policy. In response to voter dissatisfaction, Alaska's legislature took measures that pitted the Legislative branch against the judicial branch. Governor Palin was advised by her attorney general that the legislation in question was probably unconstitutional. The situation created an ethical dilemma for Sarah Palin. On one hand, she agreed with the Legislature and had made her views on homosexual marriage clear to Alaskan citizens. But on the other hand—as governor—she was sworn to uphold the state's constitution.

Palin's supporters encouraged and even pressured her to sign the bill that, in effect, would negate the Supreme Court's decision. Signing the bill would have been consistent with her personal views on the subject of same-sex marriage. But her duty to uphold the constitution weighed heavily on her. She had sworn an oath to uphold the constitution, whether she agreed with it or not. Deciding to put duty before personal preference, Governor Palin braved the wrath of her supporters and vetoed the no-benefits legislation. Predictably, she paid a heavy price for this courageous act.

Her supporters thought she was a turncoat or worse, and they made sure Sarah Palin knew how they felt. However, over time—as anger gave way to reason—Palin supporters realized that they had elected a Governor who had the courage to stand on principle even when she did not agree with the circumstances that invoked the principle. It is easy for a politician to take a stand the opposition will not like. They are elected to do precisely that. But to knowingly incur the wrath of those who put you in office and with whom you agree takes moral courage. Her supporters eventually came to realize this fact.

CHRISTIANITY

In a country founded on Christian principles and values, it has become common for politicians to deny America's Christian heritage. President Obama has gone so far as to claim that America is not a Christian nation but instead is one of the world's largest Muslim nations. He is wrong on both accounts. In a country where all religions are tolerated—except Christianity—it is refreshing to have a presidential candidate such as Sarah Palin who is honest, open, and forthright about her Christian beliefs.

Sarah Palin began life as a Catholic. Her family later left the Catholic Church and joined the Assemblies of God denomination. As an adult, Sarah Palin and her family attended the Wasilla Bible Church. After being elected governor, Sarah attended the Juneau Christian Center on those Sundays when she was in the state's capital. Beginning life in one Christian denomination and then later switching to another makes Sarah Palin like a lot of Christians in America. The ability to do so is one of the benefits of freedom of religion guaranteed to all Americans in the First Amendment. Switching from one church to another as the family's needs and beliefs changed also makes the

Palins like a lot of Americans.

What is even more refreshing about Sarah Palin is that she quietly but consistently lives out her religious beliefs, rather than just pulling them out of the closet at election time. She is not one to turn a campaign speech into a sermon. Rather, her life and how she lives it is her sermon. In America there is an unfortunate phenomenon known as the *election-time Christian*. ETCs are political candidates who make a big show of their religion for selected audiences during their campaigns and then promptly forget about religion until the next election. For Sarah Palin, religion is a way of life, not a way to get elected. Sarah Palin's faith is the deeply internalized foundation of her life.

CHANGE AGENCY

Presidents, by definition, must be change agents. One of the reasons they are elected is that the American public wants change. Presidential candidates often run for office on a platform of changing what their predecessor has done. This is why the theme of every presidential candidate, whether stated or just implied, is "Vote for me and I will make things better for you." Barack Obama became president by promising change in the most general sense—nothing specific, just "change". After he became president, people began to learn the details of his proposed "changes" and found they were no longer so enamored of his promises. In fact, many came to realize too late that when Barack Obama promised change they should have questioned him concerning the specifics.

Sarah Palin's record suggests that she understands the most fundamental rule about being a change agent. That rule is simply this: *There is only one justifiable reason for changing anything, and that is to make it better.* If the change in question will not make things better, why make the change? It is this fundamental rule of change that got President Obama in trouble with the American public on such issues as the environment, healthcare, and the economy. As long as he limited himself to broad generalizations about change, Obama's words were well-received. But once he began to reveal the specifics of the changes he wanted to make, Americans started to question whether these changes would make things better for them.

Sarah Palin has made many changes during her political career. In fact, she went into politics for the purpose of changing things for the better—first as mayor of Wasilla and then as Governor of Alaska. As mayor, she wanted to make local government more responsive and respectful of the citizens it was supposed to serve. As governor, she wanted to eliminate corruption in state government. In both cases, she succeeded. Sarah Palin's views on change can be seen best in her own words: "In politics, there are some candidates who use change to promote their careers. And then there are those...who use their careers to promote change."[9]

Sarah Palin campaigned for mayor of her hometown of Wasilla with the express purpose of bringing about badly needed change. As with many small towns, Wasilla was in need of infrastructure improvements, particularly in the areas of roads, sewers, public transportation, airport facilities, and law enforcement. Infrastructure improvements are expensive. In fact, few things trouble local elected officials more than trying to keep up with the infrastructure needs of their municipalities; and the smaller the city the bigger the challenge. This is because small towns do not have a sufficient tax base to generate the level of funding necessary to make infrastructure improvements.

Faced with the need for infrastructure improvements but lacking a sufficient tax base to generate them locally, Mayor Palin did what effective change agents must do: she thought creatively and improvised. She hired a consultant to advise the city on alternative sources of funding. Acting on the consultant's advice, Mayor Palin was able to secure funding and loans that for the most part went directly to the organizations that needed them to make the necessary infrastructure improvements. As a result, Wasilla's roads, sewer system, police department, airport, and bus system were upgraded and improved.

When Sarah Palin became Governor of Alaska, large oil companies controlled state government and corruption was rampant and widespread. In fact, federal investigators eventually concluded that a number of state legislators had actually taken bribes from the oil companies. Clearly, change was needed but it would not be made unless someone had the courage to stand up to the oil companies and their entrenched minions in the state legislature. In Sarah Palin, Alaska's citizens finally had a leader who would make the changes necessary to clean up the corruption.

In order to do this Governor Palin needed to find a way to break the stranglehold the big oil companies had on Alaska and change the way state government conducted its business. Sarah Palin had barely taken office when a challenge requiring major change presented itself. The part of Alaska in and around Prudhoe Bay contains one of the richest deposits of natural gas in the world. For the people of Alaska it amounted to buried treasure, but there was a problem: getting it out of the ground and transporting it to market.

When Palin took office, she faced a situation in which her predecessor, Frank Murkowski, had already negotiated a deal with a consortium of large oil companies to lay a pipeline from Prudhoe Bay across Canada to the lower 48 states. The deal was so controversial that the state legislature had filed a lawsuit requesting an injunction to prevent it from being consummated. The injunction was granted, and this is where things stood when Sarah Palin took office. On one hand, Murkowski's deal with the large oil companies was unpopular with Alaska's citizens, but on the other hand, getting the pipeline built appeared to be so monumental a task that only the large oil companies could get it done.

Governor Palin was faced with a Catch-22 situation. The state needed to break the stranglehold large oil companies had on government, but it also needed the revenue the natural gas of Prudhoe Bay could provide. The citizens of Alaska appeared to be held hostage by the capabilities of the large oil companies. Would Alaskans be forced to accept terms dictated to them by the oil companies in order to gain the benefits of their state's natural resources? Sarah Palin's answer to this question was, "Not if I can help it." As it turned out, she could. Rather than give in to the oil companies, Sarah Palin once again did what effective change agents always do—thought creatively and improvised.

Governor Palin did the same thing she had done as Mayor of Wasilla when she needed to find new sources of revenue to fund infrastructure improvements: she identified someone—in this case several people—who could provide her with the expertise she did not have. Palin assembled a team of experts to explore all of the various options for constructing the badly needed pipeline. Working with this team of experts, Governor Palin developed the *Alaska Gasline Inducement Act (AGIA)*. This act contained a plan based on the twin pillars of private-sector competition and government incentives. The idea behind the AGIA was to make building and operating the pipeline enticing enough that a private firm or a consortium of private firms would accept the contract, but on terms that would be good for the people of Alaska rather than big oil companies.

If Governor Palin could find a consortium of private-sector firms willing to undertake the massive project at reasonable terms, she would take a major step toward breaking the stranglehold big oil had on state government, while simultaneously ensuring that the people of Alaska would benefit from the sale of their state's resources. If Governor Palin failed, Alaska would be back to the status quo in which only the large oil companies and their handpicked minions in the state legislature would benefit.

Unwilling to admit defeat, the large oil companies announced that they would not participate in construction of the pipeline on the Governor's terms. The oil companies did not want to be part of a consortium they did not control or help complete a project on someone else's terms. Deciding to take the risk, Governor Palin called their bluff and announced that the project would proceed with or without the participation of the oil companies. By now, all Americans know who won this epic battle of wills.

A careful examination of how Sarah Palin was so successful as a change agent in her roles as Mayor of Wasilla and Governor of Alaska reveals an approach that other elected officials would do well to emulate. It consists of three specific strategies that she used to effectively implement changes that needed to be made but that were opposed by entrenched bureaucracies and powerful, well-funded political opponents. These strategies are:

- Anticipate the need for change

- Understand your role in making change happen and play the role effectively

- Have the courage to stand up to those who oppose change

Anticipate the Need for Change

One of the reasons Sarah Palin has been so effective at anticipating the need for change is her view of the purpose of government. She thinks that government exists to help people, but in carefully defined and limited ways. Consequently, when she observes that government is not serving this fundamental purpose, she knows that changes must be made.

Sarah Palin entered politics because she wanted to make city government more responsive to Wasilla's citizens. She knew first-hand how things were, and she knew how they should be. In other words, she saw the need for change before ever deciding to run for office. Sarah Palin also anticipated the need for change at the state level before deciding to run for governor. She became aware of the corruption, the subservience of state government to large oil companies, and that only a favored few were benefitting from the state's natural resources. Once again, because she thought government should serve a specific but limited purpose and did not see this happening, Sarah Palin was able to anticipate the need for change and run for office to make the needed changes.

Understand Your Role in Making Change Happen and Play the Role Effectively

One of the reasons Sarah Plain has been so effective at making changes in government policies and practices is that she understands her role in the process. A change agent rarely makes changes unilaterally, particularly in government. Rather, the role of the change agent is to: 1) anticipate changes that are needed, 2) develop a vision of how things will be better if the changes are made, 3) identify any inhibitors that might prevent the changes from being made, 4) find ways to eliminate or mitigate the change inhibitors, 5) identify people with the expertise to make the changes and gain their commitment, 6) implement the changes, and 7) monitor progress, solve any unanticipated problems that arise, and make necessary adjustments to ensure that the change takes hold.

The example of building the natural gas pipeline from Prudhoe Bay to the lower 48 mentioned earlier shows how, as governor, Sarah Palin applied all seven of these steps. By the time she was elected, Sarah Palin knew that changes were needed and one major change was how the natural gas pipeline would be constructed and operated. Her vision of how things would be better after the necessary changes were accomplished was: *a properly-functioning pipeline that efficiently delivers natural gas from Prudhoe Bay to the lower 48 while ensuring that all Alaskans benefit from it, rather than just big oil and a few hand-picked politicians.*

Governor Palin identified the oil companies as potential inhibitors that might prevent the needed changes from being made. She mitigated the inhibitors they put in her path by creatively finding a way to get the pipeline built without them. By providing carefully thought-out incentives, Governor Palin was able to find private-sector companies that could and would build and operate the pipeline on her terms and for the good of the people of Alaska. Having secured the support of the legislature, she gave her approval for the project to proceed. As construction of the pipeline ensued, Governor Palin monitored progress and worked with the contractor to iron out any unanticipated problems that arose.

Have the Courage to Stand Up to Those Who Oppose Change

Oil company executives who were accustomed to using their money and influence to get their way in Alaska were at a loss concerning how to deal with a governor who was not interested in their money or moved by their influence.

What they could not understand, at least initially, is that what Sarah Palin wanted was to regain control of state government for the people of Alaska and then use that control to improve their lives. When oil company executives found they could not buy Governor Palin, they tried to intimidate her.

Convinced that the natural gas pipeline could not be constructed without their assistance, the large oil companies refused to play any role in the construction of the pipeline on Governor Palin's terms. This threat put Sarah Palin between a rock and a hard place. On one hand, if the large oil companies followed through on their threat, the pipeline might not ever be completed, a circumstance that could well end Sarah Palin's political career. On the other hand, if she submitted to their blackmail, the large oil companies would continue to control state government in Alaska. Had the oil companies studied their adversary more carefully, they would have known better than to back Sarah Palin into a corner. Governor Palin called their bluff, as anyone who had played basketball with Sarah Barracuda could have told them she would. She went eye-to-eye with the large oil company executives, and they blinked.

COMPETITIVENESS

The race for the presidency makes all other races—the Tour de France, Iditarod, and the Boston Marathon—look easy. It is the most competitive race in the world. Only an individual who is intensely competitive will win the race to be the leader of the free world. Sarah Palin is such an individual. Competitiveness is a trait that will serve her well in the next presidential election, but it will also serve her and the United States well should Sarah Palin become president. The United States competes constantly in the global arena, and our country is the one for which all of the others are gunning. In the global arena, the United States is like the long-time Olympic champion that all the other competitors want to beat.

Sarah Palin's competitive spirit became evident early on. As a basketball player at Wasilla High School, she earned the nickname Sarah Barracuda because she was so competitive. As a member of the high school's track team, if winning could be achieved by outworking, out practicing, or out hustling her opponents, Sarah would win. Near the end of her senior year in high school, Sarah injured her ankle. It was a bad sprain that would heal only if she stayed off of it completely. This meant no more basketball; something Sarah would not accept. With her team going to the playoffs against arch-rival Robert Service High School, Sarah was determined to play. This was a make-or-break game, and as co-captain of the team, Sarah wanted to do her part to ensure a win.

In spite of her injury, Sarah played and made an important contribution to keeping her team in the game, against what was really a better team. Finally forced to sit out most of the second half because of her injury, Sarah ached—literally and figuratively—as she watched her team go back and forth with the girls from Robert Service High. Neither team could pull away, so the game remained close—a real nail-biter. Nearing the end of the game with the score tied,

Wasilla's coach called on Sarah Barracuda to get back in the game.

With her injured ankle throbbing, Sarah took the in-bounds pass and began working the ball up the court deliberately and with determination—ignoring the pain she felt with every step. As she drove to the basket, her concentration complete, Sarah was suddenly stopped short by the referee's shrill whistle. A Robert Service player had fouled her, creating one of those perfect moments in sport that will be remembered and discussed for a lifetime. As Sarah stood at the foul line, along with everyone else in the gym, she knew that the game was now in her hands. If she became faint-hearted and choked, her team would lose. But if she called on the reserves of her competitive spirit, her team just might win. As every player on both teams and everyone in the gym looked on with bated breath, Sarah went through the same preparatory motions she had practiced hundreds of time. The tension in the gym was tangible. No one dared even breathe. Calling on those skills she had developed by swallowing her pride and moving down to the junior varsity team the year before, Sarah Barracuda—the ultimate competitor—sunk both shots making her team the new state champion.

Sarah Palin brought this same level of competitiveness to all aspects of her life, but none more so than politics. When she ran for mayor, Sarah had little more to work with than a vision for making things better and her competitive spirit. When she ran for governor against an entrenched opponent backed by powerful special-interest groups, many thought Sarah had no chance. But those who played basketball or ran track with her at Wasilla High School knew better. In fact, they might have even pitied her opponents. According to one of Sarah's coaches, Roger Nelles, Sarah's nickname was appropriate. "It was a nickname that described a trait many had already seen in her personality—a stubborn, unbending determination. Once convinced she was right, Sarah would not stop until she prevailed."[10]

CREDIBILITY

Credibility is essential to effective leadership. Leaders have credibility when those they lead believe in them, trust them, and think they are competently leading in the right direction. For example, one of the reasons that Congress has so little credibility with the voting public is that it exempts itself from so many of the laws and policies it inflicts on the American people. In order to have credibility, leaders must be seen experiencing the same challenges and suffering the same pain as those they lead. While serving in the Marine Corps, my fellow non-commissioned officers and I learned that anyone who leads at any level from the smallest fire team to the largest division is expected to share the experiences of his men. We were expected to eat what they ate—but only after making sure they got enough—sleep where they slept, carry the same load they carried, march right beside them, and lead from the front. Doing these things is how a leader earns credibility.

This is why during his first year in office, President Obama's honeymoon with the American people was so brief. The more they learned about their new president, the less credibility he had. Some political pundits speculate that the credibility issue is why President Obama tried to push so much of his real agenda—as opposed to the one he campaigned on—through Congress so soon after being elected. He knew that once the American public saw him without a mask on, his ability to influence the political process would decline rapidly.

Credibility has always been a strong point for Sarah Palin. She had a high level of credibility with the people of Wasilla when serving as their mayor and with the people of Alaska when serving as their governor. One of the reasons that she has a high level of credibility with everyday Americans is that—unlike Congress—she has never been exempt from the things they have to deal with in their daily lives, nor has she chosen to exempt herself, even when she could have. This is why as soon as she took office Sarah Palin sold the governor's personal jet. The citizens of Alaska fly commercially. Hence, so would their governor. She has been a homemaker, raised children, struggled to pay the monthly bills, driven her children to ballgames, helped her husband run his business, and been a member of the PTA.

Even more importantly, like many parents—but very few members of Congress—Sarah Palin has a son (Track) serving in the military who is deployed to Iraq. Waiting, wondering, and worrying about a son's safety is not an abstract concept for Sarah Palin. She has felt the same gut-wrenching anxiety that all parents of military personnel must endure. She also knows first-hand the daily challenge of keeping a family fed. As a youngster, Sarah pulled herself out of bed before daylight many times to hunt and fish with her father so the family would have meat on the table.

Like many parents, Sarah Palin has had to face the heart-breaking dilemma of having a child become pregnant out of wedlock. This situation is difficult enough to deal with when confined to family and friends, but Sarah Palin was forced to deal with it on national television. Then, to make matters worse, Sarah and her family had to listen while unscrupulous left-wing media pundits— dedicated advocates of abortion—hypocritically attacked the Palin family's morality. But Sarah Palin had the last word when she responded to the attacks by saying: "Our family has the same ups and downs as any other, the same challenges and same joys. Sometimes the greatest joys bring challenge."[11]

These were words everyday Americans could relate to. In fact, her daughter's out-of-wedlock pregnancy and the mean-spirited attacks from the left actually, enhanced Sarah Palin's credibility with the American public. Those who had experienced a similar situation could relate to and empathize with her. Those who had not faced this situation could still admire the loving, caring, forthright manner in which Sarah and her family faced it and the strength she showed in standing up to media bias.

Sarah Palin has consistently exemplified ten traits that make her an appealing person to a broad cross-section of the American public. These same ten traits make her a viable presidential candidate if she will refuse to be leashed, muzzled, or remolded by timid advisors. These traits are clarity, character, candor, commitment, caring, courage, Christianity, change agency, competitiveness, and credibility.

NOTES

1. Joe Hilley, *Sarah Palin: A New Kind of Leader* (Grand Rapids, MI: Zondervan, 2008), 68.

2. Kenneth Kahn, "Rick Warren Reveals the Kind of Leader America Needs," *Christian Post.* Retrieved from http://www.christianpost.com/article/20080820/rick-warren-reveals-the-kind-of-leader-america-needs on August 25, 2009.

3. Yuval Levin, "The Meaning of Sarah Palin." Retrieved from https://www.commentarymagazine.com/viewarticle.cfm/the-meaning-of-sarah-palin-1467 on August 16, 2009

4. Sarah Palin, Excerpt from her acceptance speech at the Republican National Convention, St. Paul, Minnesota, September 3, 2008.

5. *Ibid.*

6. "Father: Palin Showed Grit at Early Age." CNN Network, Atlanta, Georgia, Retrieved from www.cnn.com on September 13, 2008.

7. As quoted in Joe Hilley, *Sarah Palin: A New Kind of Leader* (Grand Rapids, MI: Zondervan, 2008), 23.

8. "Same-Sex Benefits Ban Gets Palin Veto," *Anchorage Daily News,* December 29, 2006.

9. As quoted in Hilley, 95.

10. *Ibid.*

11. *Ibid.*

Two

Commit to
the Constitution

*"The Conservative is an originalist, for he believes that
much like a contract, the Constitution sets forth certain
terms and conditions for governing that hold the same
meaning today as they did yesterday
and should tomorrow."*

—Mark R. Levin
Liberty and Tyranny: A Conservative Manifesto

After at least four years of Barack Obama's domestic
and foreign policy ineptitude, the next President of
the United States will face an unprecedented number of
major challenges. These challenges will include a fragile
economy, monumental debt, energy dependence on nations that hate the U.S., a growing entitlement mentality among Americans, threats from nuclear rogue states,
a weakened intelligence system, and on-going terrorist plots. And if these issues are not sufficiently mindboggling, the next president will also face an even bigger
challenge: a battle for the very *idea* of America—what
America means and what it means to be an American.

The United States is more than just a country on a map,
it is an idea; an idea captured eloquently by Thomas Jef-

ferson in the Declaration of Independence: "We hold these truths to be self-evident, that all men are created equal, that they are endowed by their Creator with certain un-alienable Rights, that among these are Life, Liberty, and the pursuit of Happiness. That to secure these rights, Gov-ernments are instituted among Men, deriving their just powers from the consent of the governed." Precisely how the government of the United States is to be "constituted among men" and how the government is to derive its "just powers from the consent of the governed" is set forth in the Constitution.

The Constitution is under attack by people who are trying to change it in ways so drastic, that the government about which Lincoln said should be "of the people, by the people, and for the people" is being transformed into a government "of the state, by the state, and for the state". If the next president does not reverse this trend and restore the Constitution to the intent of the founders, the great experiment described by Thomas Jefferson will fail and the idea of America will die. Sarah Palin has shown herself to be the type of individual who will fight to restore the Con-stitution and, in turn, America. If she makes restoring the Constitution part of her political platform, Americans will heed the call and support her.

Battle for the Sovereignty and Integrity of the Constitution

The Constitution translates Jefferson's eloquent words from the Declaration of Independence into more specific terms, making the idea of the United States a practical reality for Americans. Unfortunately, the Constitution is under attack and it is the very idea of what it means to be an American which is at risk. Those involved in the battle for the Constitution comprise two warring camps. One camp consists of those who believe in protecting the integrity and sovereignty of the Constitution. This camp is comprised of advocates of the concept known as *originalism.* The other camp consists of those who believe the Constitution should continually change to match the continually changing socio-cultural trends in America. They further believe that international treaties and laws can be allowed to take precedence over the Constitution. This camp is comprised of advocates of the concept known as the *living Constitution.*

Originalism

Originalism refers to interpreting the Constitution in a way that is informed by, and honors, the intent or meaning of the original authors. It views the Constitution as a sovereign document that, protects the sovereignty of the American people. Originalists fall into two categories: advocates of *original intent* and advocates of *original meaning.* Original intent and original meaning advocates both believe that there is a fixed authority when it comes to interpreting the Constitution, but they differ concerning what that authority is. Original intent advocates believe that what the drafters of the Constitution meant by their words when they wrote them should be the deciding authority in matters of interpretation. Original meaning advocates believe that what a reasonable person living at the time of the drafting of the Constitution would have understood the words to mean should be the interpretative authority.

Determining the intent of the founders or the meaning of their words requires us to do something very few Americans do: study, not just the Constitution, but other founding documents such as *The Federalist Papers*. This multi-volume work contains the complete record of the debates that occurred in the Constitutional Convention and the state ratification conventions in which supporters of ratification of the Constitution had to justify its every feature against the criticisms of astute anti-Federalists, as well as others who were neither for nor against ratification. One of the reasons these crucial volumes are not taught today is that leftist professors do not want their students to know the original intentions of the framers of the Constitution.   Prominent advocates of originalism include Supreme Court Justices Antonin Scalia and Clarence Thomas. Constitutional scholar Robert Bork is also an originalist. The benefits of originalism include the following:

- Originalism gives Constitutional authority to the people governed, thus enuring the sovereignty of the governed.

- Originalism defers to the process of change established by the founders—the amendment process. The amendment process gives Americans a way to respond to socio-cultural changes while still protecting the Constitution—and in turn the

American people—from fickle societal trends.

- Originalism protects Americans from the personal agendas, values, and biases of individual judges. It constrains judicial interpretation that is biased by personal preference.

- Originalism provides stability and predictablility—two foundational legal concepts—and protects against arbitrary decisions and interpretations by judges, legislators, and presidents trying to advance a political agenda or act on personal bias.

- Originalism protects the very purpose of the Constitution—to keep judges from constantly reforming what America is and what it means to be an American.

- Originalism provides common ground for interpreting the Constitution—the original intent or the original meaning of the founders. Other approaches share no common ground and no objective or honest means for arriving at a valid interpretation.

- Originalism protects against the politicizing of the judicial branch (which was explicitly rejected by the framers but which is now a fact of life in America, precisely because of the actions and decisions of living Constitution advocates). Originalism guards against law being made by the judicial, rather than the legislative, branch by forcing judges to ask "What do the words say?" rather than "What would I like the words to say?"

- Originalism protects the sovereignty of the Constitution by ensuring that it does not become subservient to international treaties or laws.

Living Constitution

Advocates of a living Constitution believe that it is a dynamic document meant to be flexible enough to change with the times. Originalists agree that the Constitution must be able to accommodate change, but unlike living Constitution advocates they believe that the amendment process is the appropriate vehicle for changing it. When interpreting the Constitution, a living Constitution advocate will be informed more by personal bias, international law, current socio-cultural trends, and international treaties than by the meaning or intent of the founders.

There are many advocates of the living Constitution concept, primarily because it is a convenient philosophy for those who wish to use the courts to advance their own political agendas. For example, one of the more prominent advocates of the living Constitution is former vice-president Al Gore. Problems with the living Constitution concept include the following:

- It encourages judicial activism that results in laws being made by judges rather than legislators, which is a direct violation of the Constitution. This is the concept known as "legislating from the bench."

- It allows judges to make the Constitution say what they want it to, rather than what it actually says and what the founders meant it to say.

- It allows judges to simply disregard Constitutional language they do not like or do not agree with.

- It allows international law and international treaties to take precedence over the Constitution, thereby undermining the sovereignty of the Constitution.

- It allows presidents, legislators, and judges to subvert the Constitution in the name of making it a modern document.

In condemning the concept of the living Constitution, Supreme Court Justice Antonin Scalia said: "There's the argument of flexibility and it goes something like this: The Constitution is over 200 years old and societies change. It has to change with society, like a living organism, or it will become brittle and break. But you would have to be an idiot to believe that; the Constitution is not a living organism; it is a legal document. It says some things and doesn't say other things...Proponents of the living constitution want matters to be decided not by the people, but by the justices of the Supreme Court...They are not looking for legal flexibility, they are looking for rigidity, whether it's the right to abortion or the right to homosexual activity, they want that right to be embedded from coast to coast and to be unchangeable."[1]

A Brief Review of the Constitution

The United States Constitution is one of the most significant documents ever written. In fact, for Americans the three most important documents are the Holy Bible, the Declaration of Independence, and the Constitution. Known as the father of the Constitution, James Madison kept a journal of the debates that occurred during the development of the original document. From Madison's notes we can learn much, including why the framers established the Constitution's many characteristics. Writing about the framers of the Constitution, Greenburg and Page noted that "the delegates were conversant with the great works of Western philosophy and political science; with great facility and frequency, they quoted Aristotle, Plato, Locke, Montesquieu, and scores of other thinkers. They were also surprisingly young, averaging barely over 40 years of age. Finally, these delegates, who became the framers of the U.S. Constitution, had broad experience in American politics—most had served in their state legislatures—and many were veterans of the Revolutionary War."[2] According to historian Melvin Urofsky, "few gatherings in the history of this or any other country could boast such a concentration of talent."[3]

If the Declaration of Independence represents America's vision, the Constitution is the game plan for realizing that vision. Key principles in the Constitution as set forth by the founders are:

- *Republican Form of Government.* A form of government based on popular consent and popular participation, it also includes precautions against pure majoritarian democracy while also protecting against all forms of government tyranny. With Republicanism, public policies are made by representatives elected by the people, rather than directly by the people themselves as would be the case with pure majoritarian democracy. Federalist papers numbers 10 and 51 written by James Madison, describe the republican form of government, America's particular form of republican government, and the rationale for it in greater detail.

- *Selection of Government Leaders by Election.* The representatives—Congressmen, Senators, and President—that make public policy are elected by the people. Of course, in the case of the President there is the Electoral College, but the people still elect the President indirectly. This approach ensures that there is popular consent of the governed and participation by the governed while also protecting against the possibility of a tyrannical government of the few over the many.

- *Limited Federalism.* The Constitution did away with the loose confederation of states established by its predecessor, the Articles of Confederation. In its place was established a limited federal system. In this system, some powers are given to the federal government, some are forbidden to the states, some are shared by the state and federal governments, and the rest are left to the states. Article VI, Section 2, known as the "Supremacy Clause," describes the federal system it established: "This Constitution and the Laws of the United States which shall be made in Pursuance thereof; and all Treaties made, or which shall be made, under the Authority of the United States, shall be the supreme Law of the Land; and the Judges in every state shall be bound thereby, any Thing in the Constitution of Laws of any state to the contrary notwithstanding." In other words, the Constitution established a limited federal system that leans in favor of the federal government for certain specified national purposes by giving it the power to do such things as: regulate commerce, provide a uniform currency, provide uniform laws on bankruptcy, raise and support an Army and Navy, declare war, collect taxes, provide for the common defense, collect custom duties, and other powers vital to national well-being (see Article I, Section 8 for a complete listing of the federal government's powers), but leaves the majority of powers in the hands of the state governments.

• *Limited Government.* The founders made sure that they carefully defined what the government could and could not do. In other words, they envisioned limited government and developed a document to ensure that government would be

COMMIT TO THE CONSTITUTION

limited. The limitations on the federal government are contained in Article I, Sections 8 and
9, and the Bill of Rights. Article I, Section 8 lists
what the federal government *may* do. Article I,
Section 9 lists what the federal government *may
not do.* The Bill of Rights—the first ten amend-
ments to the Constitution—provide important
protections for the individual from the national
government, and protects the powers retained by
the states.

• *Barriers to Pure Majority Rule.* Concerned
about the potential abuses of pure majority
rule—for example mob rule—the founders built
several barriers into the Constitution to preclude majoritarian democracy. These barriers
or precautions include a bicameral legislative
branch (a Congress consisting of a Senate and a
House of Representatives), unelected judiciary,
limits on the powers of the federal government,
indirect election of the president (Electoral College), and various checks and balances, including federalism—a system of separation of power
and checks and balances between the state and
federal governments.

• *Separation of Powers.* The founders were concerned about misrule and excesses on the part of
all three branches of government: executive, legislative, and judicial. They solved this problem by
applying the concept of balanced government en-

visioned by the French philosopher Montesquieu. Balanced government is based on an awareness of the sinful nature of man and on the principle that it is dangerous to empower any one branch of government with too much power. This danger is overcome by dividing the various powers of government and distributing them among the various government branches (*i.e.* executive, legislative, and judicial). This separation of powers was codified in the Constitution with Article I listing the legislative powers, Article II the executive powers, and Article III the judicial powers. The founders also included various ways that the three branches of government check each other by ensuring that no branch of government can carry out its duties solely on its own. Rather, each branch requires the cooperation of the other branches. For example, the Supreme Court can declare executive acts to be unconstitutional, but the President nominates judges to the Supreme Court. Congress enacts laws, but the President can veto them. The Supreme Court can declare acts of Congress unconstitutional, but federal judges must be confirmed by the Senate, Congress controls the Supreme Court's budget, and Congress can impeach federal judges. As Federalist Number 51 and others make clear, federalism provides a double security for the rights of the people by establishing a separation of powers as well as checks and balances between the national and state governments.

We hope this brief overview of Constitutional principles provides a perspective concerning what is at stake in the battle over the sovereignty and integrity of the Constitution as presented in the remainder of this chapter.

Sovereignty of the Constitution

The Constitution was established as the supreme law of the land for the United States. No other law, treaty, or action may take precedence over the Constitution. Unfortunately, advocates of the living Constitution—including Supreme Court judges—are moving ever closer to allowing international treaties and international law to supersede the Constitution. In order for a treaty to be valid, it must conform to the Constitution because the Constitution is a higher legal authority than a treaty. The Constitution is what gives our government the legal authority to enter into treaties, a fact that protects America's sovereignty when interacting with foreign powers. The sovereignty of the Constitution protects the sovereignty of the American people, our authority to govern ourselves independent of foreign intervention.

International law consists of laws developed and ratified by other countries and organizations, which means that American citizens have no voice in their development or ratification. Consent of the governed is a fundamental principle of the Constitution. Therefore, laws that were developed and enacted without the consent of the American people should not be applied to the American people. Unfortunately, because of the misdeeds of judges, international law is finding its way into American courtrooms.

Sovereignty and International Treaties

International treaties are supposed to be subservient to the Constitution which is the source of authority for government officials who enter into treaties. Increasingly, liberal government officials are showing a propensity for putting international treaties over and above the Constitution. Examples of where the issue of Constitutional sovereignty versus international treaties has already come into play include the Montreal and Kyoto Protocols.

Montreal Protocol

The Montreal Protocol deals with reducing substances that deplete the ozone layer, principally chlorofluorocarbons (CFCs) and hydrochlorofluorocarbons (HCFCs). Certainly there is nothing wrong with wanting to protect the ozone layer. However, there is a major problem with the Montreal Protocol from a Constitutional perspective: the issue of sovereignty. This issue surfaced when an environmental group, the National Resources Defense Council (NRDC), sued the Environmental Protection Agency (EPA) for not updating its standards for a certain chemical that was thought to have a negative effect on the ozone layer.

According to Jeremy Rabkin, "There is a treaty setting the standard, and the EPA was in conformity with the treaty. But the NRDC pointed out that Congress had instructed the EPA to conform with the Montreal Protocol and its subsequent elaborations. In other words, various international conferences had called for stricter emission standards for this chemical, and Congress told the EPA to accept these new standards as a matter of course. The response to this by the D.C. Court of Appeals was to say, in effect, that it couldn't believe Congress had meant to do that, since Congress cannot delegate its Constitutional power and responsibility to legislate for the American people to an international body."[4]

Was this ceding of sovereignty the result of shoddy work on the part of Congress, a lack of understanding on the part of Congressional leaders, or an informed act taken knowingly taken on purpose? It is difficult to discern the answer to this question since Congress is known for its inattention to detail and ill-informed actions. However, there does appear to be a decline in the commitment of Congress and the courts to the concept of Constitutional sovereignty. With Barack Obama in office, this decline now also includes the executive branch.

Kyoto Protocol

The Kyoto Protocol is an amendment to an international treaty that brings countries together for the purpose of reducing global warming. The treaty is officially known as the United Nations Framework Convention on Climate Change (UNFCCC). "Countries that ratify the Kyoto Protocol agree to reduce emissions of six greenhouse gases that contribute to global warming: carbon dioxide, methane, nitrous oxide, sulfur hexafluoride, HFCs, and PFCs. The countries are allowed to use emissions trading to meet their obligations if they maintain or increase their greenhouse gas emissions. Emissions trading allows nations that can easily meet their targets to sell credits to those that cannot."[5]

President George Bush was criticized for refusing to join with other countries in ratifying the Kyoto Protocol. Instead, he offered an alternative plan for reducing greenhouse gas emissions. Bush's plan was castigated by the left, and it did have some problems. However, setting aside the details of his plan, President Bush was right philosophically. Even the United States Senate saw problems with the Kyoto Protocol. The Senate passed a resolution stating that the United States should not sign the agreement unless it included binding targets and timetables for all nations— developing and industrialized. Although the Senate was correct in the reasons it gave for passing its resolution, Senators missed the more important reason for not adopting the Kyoto Protocol—Constitutional sovereignty.

If the United States wants to comply with the standards of an international treaty such as the Kyoto Protocol, it can do so without tying itself to a consortium of foreign nations. If it does not wish to, even if it has signed a foreign treaty, there is always the question of enforcement. Submitting to an international treaty that undermines the sovereignty of the Constitution is always a mistake, even if the treaty in question is commendable, which is not to say that the Montreal and Kyoto Treaties are (there are serious problems other than the sovereignty issue with both). When the sovereignty of the Constitution is undermined, so is the sovereignty of the American people.

Sovereignty and International Law

One of the more disturbing trends in American jurisprudence is the relatively new propensity of judges to introduce international law into their decisions. According to Jeremy Rabkin, "it's another thing altogether to say that the rights of American citizens in the U.S. can be determined by foreign courts."[6] Rabkin makes the point that this practice amounts to delegating the judicial power set forth in Article 3 of the Constitution where it says judicial power "shall be vested in one Supreme Court, and in such inferior Courts as the Congress may from time to time ordain and establish."[7]

There are an increasing number of instances in which the issue of applying international law to American citizens has come into play. Perhaps the most illustrative example occurred when Spanish judges expressed their desire to arrest American politicians for war crimes if they dared visit Europe. As idiotic as this notion sounds, it is the logical extension of the concept of applying international law to American citizens. Rabkin explains the role liberal American judges and politicians have played in creating an atmosphere in which such ludicrous ideas would even be suggested: "This is preposterous. It is akin to piracy. And not only has our government not protested this nonsense, but it has contributed to building up an international atmosphere in which this sort of thing seems plausible—an atmosphere where the old idea of a jury of one's peers and the idea of Americans having rights under the Constitution give way to the notion of some hazy international standard of conduct that everyone in the world can somehow agree upon and then enforce on strangers."[8] The notion of an international standard of conduct in a world that rejects God, which has so many different religions—all with different ethical teachings and practices, and which also accommodates secular religions such as secular humanism is foolhardy. It is also antithetical to individual rights, justice, and American liberty.

Integrity of the Constitution

The integrity of the Constitution is a function of how it is interpreted by those empowered to do so. The battle over Constitutional interpretation was introduced at the beginning of this chapter as being between advocates of either originalism or the living Constitution. Only if the originalists win this battle will the integrity of the Constitution be restored. The integrity of the Constitution was on the mind of James Madison—the "father" of the Constitution—when he wrote:

> I entirely concur in the propriety of resorting to the sense in which the Constitution was accepted and ratified by the nation. In that sense alone it is the legitimate Constitution...If the meaning of the text be sought in the changeable meaning of the words composing it, it is evident that the shapes and attributes of the Government must partake of the changes to which the words and phrases of all living languages are constantly subject."[9]

Originalism tethers the decisions of judges to the original meaning of our founders. The living-Constitution approach, on the other hand, opens the judiciary to arbitrary, reckless, and self-interested decisions. American society is like a balloon floating in the air. As the winds change, the balloon will blow in that direction. As they change again, the balloon will follow suit. If it is tethered tightly to a solid stake in the ground, the balloon can endure these constant changes in the wind without blowing away, but if it is not tethered it will be lost. The Constitution is what tethers American society to the ground and originalism is what protects the tether from damage.

Living Constitution advocates like to claim that the Constitution must change to match the on-going changes in American society, but they miss an important point. Think of the Constitution as your home. Americans are constantly changing their homes—color schemes, carpet, flooring, window treatments, and furniture—to accord with changes in fashion, taste, and financial status. The reason these changes can be made without undermining the integrity of the home is the solid foundation under it. As long as the foundation under your home is solid, you can make all the changes you want. But undermine the home's foundation and the changes will one day come crashing down around you. Advocates of the living Constitution are undermining the foundation of America's sovereignty, justice, and liberty.

In his landmark book, *Liberty and Tyranny*, Mark Levin explains what is really behind the living Constitution point of view:

> The Statist considers the judiciary his clearest path to amassing authority, for through it he can proclaim what the law is without ef-

fective challenge or concern with the fleeting outcome of an election cycle. Moreover, the federal judiciary is populated with about one thousand lawyers—and the Supreme Court a mere nine—making statist infiltration easy. Even when holding high office in the executive or legislative branches, the Statist today looks for ways to enhance judicial authority at the expense of his own branch, for in doing so he seeks to immunize his agenda from a possible change in public attitudes. And the statist on the court tolerates representative government only to the extent that its decisions reinforce his ends. Otherwise, he overrules it.[10]

Obama and the Sovereignty and Integrity of the Constitution

With Barack Obama in the White House, America has never had a stronger advocate for international treaties and law. In fact, the commitments of the Obama administration made in just his first year in office suggest that the President is so concerned with his personal prestige in foreign countries that he is willing to overlook the sovereignty and integrity of the Constitution to increase it. These commitments include the following international treaties: International Gun Control Treaty (CIFTA), Anti-Counterfeiting Trade Agreement, Rights of Women and Rights of Persons with Disabilities Treaties, and a broad-based European Treaty. These examples are just the tip of the iceberg.

President Obama is a dedicated advocate of both international treaties and international law. "Barack Obama's pledge to restore the United States' international standing extends far beyond front-page topics such as closing Guantanamo and banning torture, into areas as diverse as nuclear testing, the rights of women and people with disabilities, and military and commercial activities in the world's oceans."[11]

The American Society of International Law—advocates of applying international law to American citizens—have commended President Obama for his willingness to pursue their agenda. "Observers agree that Barack Obama and Joe Biden may also reopen the doors for American support and acceptance of the International Criminal Court. Barack Obama in the past stated about the ICC that: 'The court has pursued charges only in cases of the most serious and systematic crimes and it is in America's interests that these most heinous of criminals, like the perpetrators of the genocide in Darfur, are held accountable. These actions are a credit to the cause of justice and deserve full American support and cooperation.' Advocates for American ratification of The Rome Statute of the International Criminal Court have expressed confidence in the possibility that this ratification could happen during the next four years."[12]

In other words, the advocates of ignoring Constitutional sovereignty and applying international law to American citizens are pleased to have Barack Obama in the White House. The quote from the previous paragraph about pursuing the most heinous criminals such as those who perpetrated genocide is nothing but political double-speak and misdirection by the master of both—Barack Obama. If the issue of international law were about nothing more than prosecuting perpetrators of genocide, few would argue with it. But you will notice that the President conveniently avoided such inconvenient issues as Constitutional sovereignty.

Americans are right to be suspicious about trusting the jurisprudence of other countries. For example, consider the case of Abdel Baset al-Megrahi, the Libyan terrorist who blew up Pan Am Flight 103 over Lockerbie, Scotland killing 270 people, including several Americans. Al-Megrahi was convicted in 2001 and sentenced to life in prison. However, the Scottish government released him in 2009 after he had served just eight years. This convicted murderer of 270 people was allowed to return to Libya where he was welcomed home as a hero. President Obama lodged a half-hearted pro forma protest saying he "deeply regretted" Scotland's decision. Predictably, the Scottish legal system and government paid no attention to the President's tepid comments.

Herein can be seen another problem with international treaties and laws—not only can they undermine the sovereignty of the Constitution, they are unenforceable. Nevertheless, international treaties and law have an ardent supporter in Barack Obama and their advocates in America and abroad are pleased. They finally have an American president who shares their views. Consent of the governed is a fundamental principle in a Republican Democracy, a fact that cannot be repeated too often. Applying international law to American citizens amounts to subjecting them to laws they have not consented to nor had a voice in establishing. This is an abuse similar to taxation without representation.

What the Sovereignty and Integrity Issues Mean to Sarah Palin

Even Americans who are not well-versed in the intricacies of the Constitution are put off by the specter of international treaties and international law being imposed on them. Americans have always had an inherent suspicion of "entangling alliances" with foreign countries. For many Americans, getting involved in the business of foreign countries is bad enough, but letting them get involved in ours is downright unacceptable. This inherent mistrust of letting other countries influence what happens in America will work in Sarah Palin's favor if she does the following:

- Makes the sovereignty and integrity of the Constitution an issue in the next election.

- Points out just a few instances in which international treaties and international law might impinge on the liberty of individual Americans.

- Points out how the living Constitution approach to Constitutional interpretation is actually undermining the integrity of the Constitution.

- Promises to appoint judges that adhere strictly to the concept of originalism.

• Works to help elect Senators who will support her nominations of judges who are strict originalists.

• Holds Barack Obama responsible for all of his actions that might undermine the sovereignty and integrity of the Constitution.

NOTES

1. Peter Lattman, "Scalia Assails Living Constitutionalists," *Wall Street Journal Law Blog,* February 14, 2006. Retrieved from http://blogs.wsj.com/law/2006/02/14/scalia-calls-living-consti-tutionalists-idiots/ on March 11, 2007.

2. Edward S. Greenburg and Benjamin I. Page, *America's Democratic Republic,* 3rd edition (New York: Longman, Pearson, 2009), 31-32.

3. Melvin I. Urofsky, *A March of Liberty* (New York: Knopf, 1988), 89.

4. Jeremy Rabkin, "The Constitution and American Sovereignty," *Imprimis,* July/August 2009, Volume 38, Number 7/8, 3.

5. Larry West, "Should the United States Ratify the Kyoto Protocol?" *About.com, Environmental Issues.* Retrieved from http://environment.about.com/od/kyotoprotocol/i/kyotoprotocol.htm on September 9, 2009.

6. Rabkin, 3.

7. *Ibid.*

8. *Ibid,* 4.

9. James Madison, "Letter to Henry Lee, June 25, 1824," as quoted in *The Quotable Founding Fathers: A Treasury of 2,500 Wise and Witty Quotations from the Men and Women who Created America,* ed. Buckner F. Melton, Jr. (Dulles, Virginia, Brassey's: 2004), 48.

10. Mark R. Levin, *Liberty and Tyranny: A Conservative Manifesto* (NY: Threshold Editions, 2009), 40.

11. Bob Egelko, "Obama pledge on treaties a complex undertaking." Retrieved from http://www.sfgate.com/cgi-bin/article.cgi?f=/c/a/2008/12/01/MNK414CTFB.DTL on September 10, 2009.

12. Phillip Barea, "Obama to Promote International Law and Diplomacy," *Suite 101*, November 6, 2008. Retrieved from http://international-politics.suite101.com/article.cfm/obama_to_promote_international_law on September 10, 2009.

Three

REJECT SOCIALISM

*"Those who fought to create this new country believed
in limited government with unlimited potential for its
citizens. Capitalism was the key. By letting free markets
work and keeping government out of the way, Americans
have the opportunity to grow as much as their drive,
determination, and intellect will take them.
That is the American way."*

—Bobby Eberle
The Loft, April 10, 2009

One of the first things you notice about Sarah Palin is her entrepreneurial spirit, positive work ethic, and commitment to capitalism. This commitment will be an important factor in the next presidential election. After four years of President Obama's socialist economic programs and government handouts that encourage unproductive people to think they are entitled to what others work hard to earn, Americans will be ready for a president who appreciates capitalism, entrepreneurship, and the work ethic.

America became an economic superpower not by accident, chance, or luck but because it was blessed with a capitalist economy, entrepreneurs who thrived in a free-market environment, and people with a positive work ethic who asked for nothing but the opportunity to better their circumstances. Entrepreneurship is about identifying a need, developing an idea to meet that need, and braving the risks involved to transform the idea into a business. America's history is replete with the inspiring stories of successful entrepreneurs. John Deere was such an individual. His story illustrates what is wrong with President Obama's worldview as it relates to economics.

John Deere was a blacksmith in Middlebury, Vermont when financial problems led him to sell his shop and relocate to Grand Detour, Illinois. Setting up shop in America's agricultural heartland, Deere soon had plenty of work. But he noticed a problem. The cast iron plow that worked so well in the sandier soil of Vermont did not work well in the thicker, stickier loam of Illinois. This thicker soil of America's heartland would stick to cast iron plows forcing farmers to stop plowing and clean off their plow blades so frequently that productivity suffered. Deere saw a need and decided to do something about it. Through experimentation, Deere came to the conclusion that a plow made out of highly-polished steel would work better in the sticky soil of Illinois.

The eventual result was Deere's self-scouring plow. Deere's invention grew into a company that became one of the premiere manufacturers of farm equipment in the world, and still is. This is the entrepreneurship side of the story. Deere's achievements would be legion if they just stopped with his plow and the resulting company, but this is only half of the story. In addition to creating a company and hundreds of jobs, the self-scouring plow allowed farmers with a positive work ethic to do more work in less time, increase their yields, make a better living for themselves and their families, and provide consumers with more food at lower prices.

Coupling Deere's invention with old-fashioned, roll-up-your-sleeves hard work, farmers turned the American Midwest into the most productive agricultural region in the world. This is the work ethic half of the story. What John Deere's story shows is that a free-market economy encourages the entrepreneurial spirit and traditional work ethic, empowering people to go as far as their initiative, drive, and ambition will take them. Sarah Plain not only understands this concept, she exemplifies it.

The farmers who rushed to take advantage of the self-scouring plow had a positive work ethic, an attitude based on such values as thrift, diligence, self-reliance, self-discipline, responsibility, accountability, deferred gratification, and hard work. The combination of entrepreneurs like John Deere and farmers with a positive work ethic empowered by a capitalist economy is what eventually made America an economic superpower. John Deere's invention and the farmers who benefitted from it, taken together, are the story of America. Consequently, anything that threatens America's capitalist economy, entrepreneurial spirit, or work ethic must be rejected.

Sarah Palin is a capitalist with an entrepreneurial spirit and a positive work ethic. More than just understanding the American story, Sarah Palin—like John Deere—is an example of it. But that story is being threatened by the socialist tendencies of the Obama administration. The

President's economic policies are socialistic rather than capitalistic; and his government bailouts, handouts, and entitlements undermine the entrepreneurial spirit and traditional work ethic. His call for increased government regulation, appointment of "czars" who have dictatorial powers over various sectors of the economy, multiplication of the national debt, and decisions that will result in unprecedented inflation have sent unmistakable signals that the Obama administration is hostile to free markets, capitalism, entrepreneurship, and the traditional work ethic. Under the Obama administration, Americans are learning that such values as thrift, diligence, self-reliance, self-discipline, responsibility, accountability, deferred gratification, and hard work are no longer important. Instead they are learning to look to the government for all their needs while selfishly looking out for number one. If this trend is not reversed, America is destined to go the way of Great Britain, France, and Germany—once powerful countries that are now socialist states with second-tier economies.

Americans have begun to sense that President Obama lured them down a one-way street to disaster with a stimulus plan that did not stimulate, bailouts that turned out to be handouts, and numerous other ill-advised economic strategies that have created ten-trillion dollars in debt over a ten-year period for the United States. The next president will have to commit to reversing course before it is too late. Consequently, Sarah Palin will have to commit to restoring capitalism, the entrepreneurial spirit, and the traditional work ethic. This is a commitment Americans are likely to welcome.

Socialism Gains a Foothold in America through the Entitlement Mentality

Our country's economic underpinnings are being steadily eroded by the increasing level of taxation required to fund an already bloated, but still expanding and self-perpetuating government. Because of a steadily-growing list of bailouts, handouts, and entitlements, many Americans have come to view government as the solution to their problems, rather than the source of them. This dangerously misguided perspective only serves to promote an entitlement mentality in a country that historically has been recognized for its industriousness.

To understand just how out-of-control government growth and spending are in America, consider the burgeoning cost of government. In the early 1900s, local, state, and federal government combined accounted for just seven percent of America's Gross Domestic Product (GDP). By the turn of the 20th century government consumed almost 30 percent of the GDP. This means that every third dollar in the American economy is siphoned off by government— where it is seldom put to good use—and, as a result, is not available to the private sector for productive use. In 2009, the Obama administration, with its multi-trillion dollar budget and correspondingly out-of-control deficit took the GDP hostage and transformed the federal government into a giant non-profit corporation swimming in debt. This is when the cancer of socialism that had been slowly creeping into all aspects of American life suddenly shifted into high gear, accelerating at an alarming rate.

At the same time, the entrepreneurial spirit and traditional work ethic were slowly but surely being supplanted by an entitlement mentality—a mentality that is the cornerstone of socialism. The disease of entitlement is antithetical to everything that made America great.   Worse yet, it is self-inflicted. The entitlement mentality originated in homes where overindulgent parents—also known as helicopter parents—gave their children everything they could possibly need except what they needed most: a belief in thrift, diligence, self-reliance, self-discipline, responsibility, accountability, deferred gratification, and hard work.

Children who were raised in this kind of environment grew up to become entitled adults who expect the federal government to replace their parents in providing for their every want and whim.   Consequently, when the government obliges—in the form of bailouts, handouts, and entitlements—the entrepreneurial spirit and traditional work ethic are eroded further and the diseases of socialism and entitlement become more resistant to a cure.

Socialism is More Than Just a Misguided Economic System

An economist will define socialism as a centrally planned economy in which the government controls the means of production and distribution.   This is a somewhat sterile definition similar to defining inoperable cancer as an illness. Socialism is much more than just an economic system. It is a worldview based on the premise that the state knows best what you should think and how you should live. Socialism seeks government control of all aspects of the individual's life, and uses the power of government to reduce productive, contributing people to the same level as those who are less productive and contribute little or nothing. This is what Barack Obama means when he blithely talks about "fairness" and "redistributing wealth."

With socialism, the state is supreme and all problems have the same solution: government. In a socialist system, responsibility is replaced by an aversion to responsibility, and charity is replaced by government entitlements. A government entitlement is charity by force, which is not charity at all. It is legalized theft. When the state becomes supreme and government becomes the solution, the entrepreneurial spirit, work ethic, freedom, and liberty quickly become casualties. America has contracted the disease of socialism and there is already evidence that freedom, liberty, entrepreneurship, and the work ethic are suffering the effects of it. This is a point that Sarah Palin will need to drive home to all Americans during her campaign for the presidency.

Due in part to the erosion of the entrepreneurial spirit and traditional work ethic, American businesses are struggling. By 2009, layoffs, bankruptcies, foreclosures, furloughs, idle inventory, and plant closings had become so commonplace that images of the Great Depression came easily to mind. After enjoying decades of economic prosperity, America fell on hard times. Although poor leadership, bad management, and questionable decision-making on the part of business executives have contributed to America's economic woes, the bigger culprit is the federal government. The Obama administration's response to America's economic problems is pushing our country deeper and deeper into the murky swamp of socialism where restrictions on individual freedom are the norm, the entrepreneurial spirit is drowned in bureaucratic muck, and the traditional work ethic is replaced by an entitlement mentality.

Government Culpability in America's Economic Woes

Economist Walter Williams summarizes the government's culpability in America's economic woes as follows: "Starting with the Community Reinvestment Act of 1977, which was given more teeth during the Clinton administration, Congress started intimidating banks and other financial institutions into making loans, so-called subprime loans, to high-risk homebuyers and businesses. The carrot offered was that these high-risk loans would be purchased by the government-sponsored enterprises Fannie Mae and Freddie Mac...Anyone with an ounce of brains would have known that this was a prescription for disaster...The financial collapse of Fannie Mae and Freddie Mac is not a failure of the free market, because lending institutions in a free market would not have taken on the high-risk loans. They were forced to by the heavy hand of government."[1]

Williams continues: "The solution is not a taxpayer-financed bailout. The solution is to let those who purchased homes they couldn't afford suffer the losses. Of course that takes a level of political courage that is in short supply."[2] Williams is saying that government is not the solution to America's economic woes—it is the problem. Viewing government as the solution creates an entitlement mentality that chips away at the entrepreneurial spirit and work ethic of a nation until eventually the number of people content to ride in the nation's economic wagon exceeds the number willing to pull it.

Most Critical Step in Rejecting Socialism

The most critical step in curing America's socialism disease is to properly diagnose the problem. We must understand that the problem is primarily one of character and secondarily one of economics. This is a key point that Sarah Palin will need to make part of her rhetoric during the next presidential election. Walter Williams expressed this view when he wrote: "Most of our nation's great problems, including our economic problems, have as their root decaying moral values."[3] The factors that placed our country on the slippery slope to socialism relate more to character than to economics.

America got itself into economic trouble not because it mishandled its finances. Rather, America mishandled its finances because—aided and abetted by big government—Americans lost their moral bearings. In the process, the values that historically represented critical points on America's moral compass—thrift, diligence, self-reliance, self-discipline, responsibility, accountability, deferred gratification, and hard work—were supplanted by an entitlement mentality. These values, when taken together, are the foundation of the entrepreneurial spirit and the traditional work ethic which, in turn, are the best antidotes to the entitlement mentality. Consequently, the first step in reversing America's downhill slide into socialism is to reestablish these values. Because she personifies these values, Sarah Palin has the credibility to encourage Americans to adopt and exemplify them.

These values are important enough to become part of the rhetoric of Sarah Palin's campaign for president and so are explained in more detail here:

- *Thrift.* At one time, Americans would scrimp and save to buy the things they wanted but could not afford. In those bygone days, savings accounts were common and layaway was standard practice. But with the advent of credit cards, Americans who wanted to *supersize* their lives adopted a buy-now-and-worry-about-it-later attitude. This attitude and the ease of buying on credit institutionalized the practice of living beyond one's means. As a result, Americans are drowning in a sea of debt with little hope of paying it off.

- *Diligence.* Pride of workmanship used to be an indigenous American trait. A popular maxim in years past was: *anything worth doing is worth doing right.* However, over the years, pride of workmanship has been replaced by a lax attitude that led to the coining of another maxim, one far less admirable: *it's good enough for government work.*

- *Self-reliance.* In years past, self-reliance was as American as baseball. Our country was able to span the continent from the Atlantic to the Pacific only because early Americans were a self-reliant breed. *Do it yourself* was a popular maxim that illustrated the typical American's attitude toward the everyday challenges of life. However, the teaching of socialistic doctrine in America's colleges, universities, and public schools, the overindulgence of helicopter parents, and the rapid expansion of the service sector combined to create a dependent generation that grew accustomed to having others do for them what they should do for themselves. The logical extension of this attitude is to become dependent on the government rather than on individual initiative.

• *Self-discipline.* Americans used to be a more self-disciplined society. They patiently saved for things they could not yet afford, made meals from scratch, and dressed up for church and other special occasions. Self-discipline has since been replaced by a self-centeredness in which Americans demand immediate gratification for their every want and whim. Credit cards, fast food, and other innovations that eliminate waiting, combined with an attitude that says "it's-all-about-me," have undermined self-discipline in America. Why save up for something when you can have it right now with just the swipe of a credit card? Why not purchase more house than you can afford when the government will bail you out if you default on the payments? Why make meals from scratch when you can get them in seconds at a drive-thru window? Why call

someone back later when you can simply answer
your cell phone right now, even if you are in the
middle of a movie or a meeting? Why worry
about the problems a lack of self-discipline will
create when the government will bail us out and
pass those problems on to future generations?
Finally, if it's all about me why should I worry
about self-discipline in the first place—why not
just do what I want when I want?

- *Responsibility and accountability.* Responsibility and accountability used to be hallmark
American traits. President Harry Truman made
the concepts part of America's lexicon with his
famous slogan: "The buck stops here." Unfortunately, the buck no longer stops here for many
Americans. Rather than accept responsibility,
the typical approach has become to blame someone else. People are no longer shamed by having
unpaid bills or unfulfilled obligations. In years
past when Americans saw someone in trouble
they would ask, "How can I help?" Now they are
more likely to say, "I don't want to get involved."
These days no matter how irresponsible people
might be in their choices or actions, they can
still find a way to blame someone else. In fact,
aided and abetted by an out-of-control legal
system, Americans have turned avoiding responsibility into an industry. If you buy a cup of
steaming hot coffee at a fast food-restaurant and
carelessly spill it in your lap, you are not respon-

sible. Point the finger of blame at the restaurant and sue. If you smoke cigarettes all of your life and contract lung cancer, you are not responsible. Point the finger of blame at the cigarette manufacturer and sue. If you over-eat all of your life, never exercise, and have an obesity-induced heart attack, you are not responsible. Point the finger of blame at the grocery store and sue. "It's not my fault" has become a mantra in a country that used to say "the buck stops here."

• *Deferred gratification.* There was a time before the days of no-interest loans and the ubiquitous credit card when Americans saved up for purchases they wanted to make but could not yet afford. To accommodate this thrifty approach, retailers invented the concept of layaway, and it served Americans well for decades. In addition, Americans used to believe that patience was a virtue. But now access that is 24/7/365 coupled with the ability of computers, the Internet, and cellular phones to respond instantly has eliminated much of the perceived need to wait. Unfortunately, no matter how beneficial time-saving technologies may be, they also have a down side. A negative aspect of time-saving technologies is that they contribute to a growing spirit of impatience that undermines the self-discipline needed to exercise deferred gratification. This impatience is showing up in ways that are detrimental to society (*e.g.* out-of-control credit spending, road rage, people answering cellular phones at inappropriate times, customers demanding everything right now, people eating too many unhealthy fast-food meals, the stress created when people want others to respond immediately in the manner of computers, etc.). In American politics this has shown up in demands that Congress "do something" immediately, rather than carefully consider proposed legislation; pass 1,000-page bills without reading them; spend trillions of dollars; and raise taxes to pay for the supposed benefits of the unread legislation.

• *Hard work.* Historically, Americans have been among the hardest working people in the world. A positive work ethic—derived largely from religious beliefs—ensured that Americans of previous generations worked hard. Unfortunately, hard work no longer appeals to many Americans. Contemporary generations would rather stake their economic security on government entitlements and their dreams of living the good life on winning the lottery, rather than on working hard to succeed. Working smart, which was originally intended to be a strategy for becoming more productive, is now viewed as a strategy for working less. The attitude of many Americans toward work these days is summarized in the following question: "Why should I work when the government will take care of me?"

The erosion of such traditional American values as thrift, diligence, self-reliance, self-discipline, responsibility, accountability, deferred gratification, and hard work led to the types of behaviors that brought about America's economic implosion. Out-of-control credit buying, personal and corporate greed, and government programs that reward irresponsibility—in other words, a lack of character at the individual, corporate, and government levels—led to America's economic woes. Consequently, only by restoring the values that made this country great will America be able to find permanent solutions to its economic problems.

The socialist response to economic problems only forestalls the inevitable by kicking the can down the road to be dealt with by our children and grandchildren. Although this approach may be politically expedient in the short run, in the long run it will be economically disastrous. Bail out a leaky boat and apply temporary patches to the holes and you might make it to shore this time. But in the long run what have you accomplished? If you do not permanently fix the leaks, the boat will eventually sink, taking you and its occupants down with it. America's economy is like a leaky boat and the socialistic government programs of the Obama administration are flimsy patches that are already showing signs of water damage.

A permanent solution to our country's economic problems must begin with a grassroots restoration of the values that once made us the most productive nation in the world. These values are thrift, diligence, self-reliance, self-discipline, responsibility, accountability, deferred gratification, and hard work, values that are now harder to find in America than a selfless politician. These values are the bedrock elements of the entrepreneurial spirit and traditional work ethic. They are the values that helped make America an economic superpower, and they are the values needed to overcome the entitlement mentality; a necessary first step in restoring our nation's economic strength.

The Declining Work Ethic and America's Economic Woes

Government bailouts, handouts, and entitlements will not solve America's economic problems because they do not and cannot eliminate the cause of the problems. Even a Management 101 student knows that in order to solve a problem, you must first identify and eliminate its cause. We suggest that the fundamental cause of America's economic collapse is twofold: 1) decline of the entrepreneurial spirit, and 2) decline of the traditional work ethic at all levels—executives, managers, employees, and people who should be working but aren't. Our premise is that America's downhill slide into socialism cannot be reversed without: 1) electing a president who believes in capitalism, entrepreneurship, and the traditional work ethic, and 2) committing to restoring the traditional values that are the foundation of capitalism, entrepreneurship, and the work ethic. These values include thrift, diligence, self-reliance, self-discipline, responsibility, accountability, deferred gratification, and hard work. Unlike Barack Obama, Nancy Pelosi, and Harry Reid, Sarah Palin personifies these values and, therefore, has the credibility necessary to lead the American public in restoring them.

Effects of a Declining Entrepreneurial Spirit and Traditional Work Ethic

General Motors (GM) is an illustrative example of what happens when entrepreneurship and the traditional work ethic decline. GM had already been in a long downhill spiral well before petitioning the federal government for a bailout in 2008. In fact, GM had been losing market-share to foreign competitors for decades before finally getting to the point of desperation and seeking government assistance. In the 1950s and 60s, GM was so dominant a global force that the popular saying of the time—"What's good for General Motors is good for the USA"—was no exaggeration. Then in the 1980s, with the help of American quality guru W. Edwards Deming, Japanese automobile manufacturers began to chip away at GM's marketshare (as well as that of Ford and Chrysler). Within a decade, Japanese automobile manufacturers—led by Toyota and Honda—were producing high-quality automobiles and were challenging the global primacy of GM.

By the time GM petitioned the government for a bailout in 2008, Toyota had already become the world's largest automobile maker. Unfortunately, even government bailouts in the billions could not prevent GM's inevitable decision to petition the bankruptcy courts for reorganization as a last ditch strategy for staving off insolvency. Congressman Tom Price of Georgia summarized the situation accurately when he said: "Today's U.S. auto industry lacks the dexterity to compete in the global marketplace. Even in better times, automakers have shown an inability to flourish—or even turn a profit. General Motors, for example, lost more than $51 billion from 2005 to 2007, a period of steady growth for the U.S. economy. Rather than re-evaluating their operations, automakers and organized labor received billions in federal funds. With failing business models still in place, is there any reason to believe this bailout will revitalize the industry's economic future for the long term?"[4] Congressman Price is right. The ill-advised, un-Constitutional government bailouts given to GM were like water poured into a leaky bucket. The billions of dollars intended to save the company leaked out as fast as the government could pour them in.

Although poor planning, questionable decisions, and a lack of entrepreneurial thinking on the part of management certainly contributed to the company's decline, the fundamental issue at the core of GM's problems is the concept of *superior value*, a foundational aspect of economic competition. Any business, regardless of type, survives and thrives by offering its customers products of superior value. Superior value is a combination of superior quality, superior cost, and superior service. If it consistently provides superior value, a business will prevail over its competitors, foreign and domestic. This is why the entrepreneurial spirit and traditional work ethic are so important. One of the key elements in providing products of superior value is personnel at all levels—executives, managers, and employees—who think entrepreneurially about continual improvement and who personify the traditional American work ethic.

One of the reasons that GM failed to provide superior value for its customers was the decline of entrepreneurial thinking and the work ethic among its executives, managers, and employees. Complacency, greed, intellectual laziness, misplaced confidence, and sloth combined to bring GM to its knees. Consider the example of GM's union employees.

While automotive workers in Japan and Korea were behaving like internal entrepreneurs focused on continually improving quality, cost, and service, GM's workers focused solely on getting more pay and better benefits for less work. In addition, they demanded and received a break-the-bank retirement plan that was an anchor around the neck of GM as it struggled to stay afloat in a sea of global competitors. At a time when GM needed personnel who believed in and applied the values of thrift, diligence, self-reliance, self-discipline, responsibility, accountability, deferred gratification and hard work, what they got instead was union employees with an entitlement mentality who believed that GM owed them a living from cradle to grave. President Obama's socialist economic programs encourage all Americans to adopt the same attitude.

This is why giving American businesses bailouts will not solve their problems. It is a classic Catch-22 situation. Money cannot buy an entrepreneurial spirit or a positive work ethic, but American businesses cannot out-perform their foreign competitors unless their personnel at all levels have these things. Giving a business a bailout without first correcting the shortcomings that drove it into insolvency is like pouring water into a leaky bucket without first repairing the holes. Turning control of businesses over to a federal government known far and wide for its unmatched inefficiency is like handing the keys of your car to a drunk.

America became an economic superpower not because of the federal government, but in spite of it and because Americans at all levels had an entrepreneurial spirit and a work ethic that encouraged thrift, diligence, self-reliance, self-discipline, responsibility, accountability, deferred gratification, and hard work. This message must be one of the themes of Sarah Palin's presidential campaign.

Too many Americans in today's workplace are like the boxing champion who becomes so accustomed to winning that he deludes himself into thinking he is entitled to his crown. In this state of entitled complacency he stops training and loses his edge. The predictable next step is that the complacent champion loses his crown to another fighter who is hungry, disciplined, and diligent. The attitude of this soon-to-be-dethroned champion is known as an *entitlement mentality*. In the long run, socialistic programs in the form of government bailouts, handouts, and entitlements only serve to encourage an entitlement mentality and further undermine capitalism, the entrepreneurial spirit, and America's work ethic.

The Work Ethic's Effect on Other Aspects of Life

Sarah Palin's work ethic is well-known. As a youngster, she climbed out of bed before dawn to accompany her father on hunting trips so her family would have meat on the table. As a high school athlete, she was known for outworking the competition. As an elected official, she ran campaigns and then served in office while raising a family and helping her husband with the family's business ventures. Sarah Palin personifies the entrepreneurial spirit and traditional American work ethic. Her example will be important in the next presidential election because not only will she need to exemplify these twin pillars of capitalism, she will have to convince some Americans who have grown accustomed to riding in the wagon to jump out of it and start pulling.

The traditional work ethic is important to America's recovery because it affects all aspects of a person's life, not just the work-related aspects. An individual's work ethic is part of a broader worldview that determines how he lives every aspect of his life. An individual with a positive work ethic will conduct his life much differently than one who thinks he is entitled to whatever he wants. A positive work ethic applies to all aspects of an individual's life. Unfortunately, so does an entitlement mentality. Further, just as the entrepreneurial spirit and traditional work ethic complement each other in ways that are beneficial to society, socialism and the entitlement mentality reinforce each other in ways that are detrimental.

For examples of how the work ethic applies to the non-work aspects of our lives, consider the issues of out-of-control credit card purchases and questionable mortgages, both serious problems which have contributed to the undermining of America's economy. An individual with a positive work ethic would not max out multiple credit cards or take out a mortgage he could not possibly afford because this type of behavior would violate the thrift, self-reliance, self-discipline, responsibility, accountability, and delayed gratification aspects of his worldview. If Americans had not turned away from these fundamental values, they would not have done the types of things that directly contributed to our country's economic woes.

A financial institution cannot make what has come to be known as a *liar's loan* to an individual who will not accept one. A bank cannot convince people who believe in paying cash for their everyday necessities to over-extend themselves with credit-card purchases. Merchants, no matter how adept at marketing, cannot convince people who believe in living within their means to buy more than they can afford or things they do not need. The lesson in these examples is clear. The values that undergird the traditional work ethic, if consistently applied by individual Americans, would have prevented most of the behavior now associated with America's economic doldrums.

People with a positive work ethic will apply its various elements to all aspects of their lives. It is important to grasp this point if America is going to divorce itself from socialism and the entitlement mentality. An individual with a positive work ethic views the problems he faces on a daily basis differently than one who has an entitlement mentality. Consider the issue of pursuing a college education. A person with a positive work ethic who wants to go to college but cannot afford it will think: "I am going to have to find a job that will allow me to work my way through college." A person with an entitlement mentality will think: "I need to apply for federal financial aid and government-backed student loans." The former sees paying for college as his responsibility, the latter thinks someone else should pay for it. That someone else, of course, is the American taxpayer.

People who lack a positive work ethic—those with an entitlement mentality—approach all problems from the perspective of what someone else can do for them because they think they are entitled. An individual with an entitlement mentality feels no shame in failing to pay bills or make good on promises. After all, why worry about these things when your perspective on life can be summarized in just three words: *I am entitled.* People who have an entitlement mentality are takers. They feel entitled to ride in the economic wagon. People who have a positive work ethic are contributors. They know that the wagon must be pulled and feel responsible for helping pull it.

The entitlement mentality is a critical factor that led to America's economic problems, and, even now, is contributing to our country's courtship with socialism. Hence, the entitlement mentality must be eliminated and replaced by the entrepreneurial spirit and traditional work ethic if America is going to make a real and permanent economic recovery. You do not cure a drug addict by giving him more drugs or an alcoholic by giving him drinks. These truths were illustrated in stark terms in 2009 when highly-paid business executives who had driven their companies to the brink of financial ruin used government bailouts to award themselves multi-million dollar bonuses. Reward irresponsibility and sloth, and you will get irresponsibility and sloth. This is precisely what socialism does and it is why government bailouts, handouts, and entitlements cannot solve America's economic problems.

Why Should I Work?

When the first round of government bailouts was announced in 2008, I (David Goetsch) thought back to a conversation which had taken place in my office only a week earlier. A young man who had lost his job in banking was planning to enroll for retraining at the college where I was vice-president. He had come to me seeking advice. This former banker had just gotten his first unemployment check and was obviously pleased with the concept of being paid while not working. He was also delighted to have learned how much money the federal government would provide him as a full-time student entitled to a Pell Grant.

When I started to tell this young man about some of the short-term training programs that were available to people in his position—people who needed to get back to work as quickly as possible—he stopped me in mid sentence and said: "I'm not interested in short-term training. I want to string out this college option as long as possible." Then with a conspiratorial wink, he said: "Why should I work when the government will pay me for not working?" This is a young man who had worked full-time for almost ten years and had been a productive employee. I was amazed and disturbed to see how quickly government handouts could convert a previously productive person into an entitled slacker who delighted in milking the system for all he could get out of it.

Without knowing it, this young man had illustrated the most detrimental aspect of socialist entitlement programs. Nothing can undermine an individual's entrepreneurial spirit and work ethic faster than relieving him of personal responsibility. If the government will do it for me, why should I do it for myself? If others will take care of me, why should I take care of myself? If I can ride in the wagon, why should I help pull it? Even people with a positive work ethic are susceptible to this type of thinking. This is why it is so important to reject socialism and restore capitalism, the entrepreneurial spirit, and the traditional work ethic.

Entitlement Mentality and the Me-Generation

The Me-Generation consists of people born after the mid-1970s. Although individuals of all ages can develop an entitlement mentality, members of the Me-Generation have been more prone to do so than previous generations. Unlike their predecessors, Me-Geners were raised in circumstances that encouraged the development of an entitlement mentality. Over-indulgent parents, the self-esteem movement and the teaching of socialist dogma in education, and the entertainment industry with its constant message of *it's all about you,* are bound to have an effect on the attitudes of young people.

If during your formative years someone had provided for your every want and whim while requiring nothing of you, it is reasonable to assume that you might have developed an entitlement mentality. When children who are over-indulged throughout their formative years become adults, the transition from depending on parents to depending on the government is a logical next step. This transfer of dependence from parents to the government has been the pattern for Me-Geners.

Me-Geners were given advantages their parents never had, but were required to contribute nothing to their family's well-being. If Sarah Palin's father had been like the parents of today's Me-Geners, he would not have had Sarah get out of bed before dawn on those freezing-cold mornings and accompany him on hunting trips. Rather, she would have been allowed to remain snug and warm beneath the covers of her bed while he did all the work. Fortunately for her and America, Sarah Palin's parents were not the type to raise entitled children.

Brought up in an environment where they were protected from the realities of life, told repeatedly how special they were, and given every possible material advantage, Me-Geners came to believe they were entitled. They grew accustomed to the material comfort their parents provided and eventually learned to take it for granted. Little wonder then that the entrepreneurial spirit and traditional American work ethic have been replaced by an entitlement mentality in so many Americans. To make matters even worse, what over-indulgent parents started, the government has been reinforcing through its socialist programs.

As it gained a foothold in American culture, the entitlement mentality began to manifest itself in a variety of ways. Young people who thought they deserved material success and wanted it right now started consuming and accumulating on the basis of easy credit. Why work long and hard to save up for something when you can have it right now with just the swipe of a plastic card? Why not purchase a house well above your income bracket when easy credit is so readily available? Why work your way through college when government-backed student loans and grants are there for the asking?

As the entitlement mentality gained momentum in America, credit card debt, ill-advised consumer loans, and questionable home-mortgages skyrocketed. In addition, government-backed student loans to pay for college degrees in subjects that have only marginal payback potential became commonplace. To make matters even worse, the entitlement mentality began to have a detrimental effect on productivity. While Americans were supersizing their lives and living beyond their means, productivity in the workplace was declining.

Beginning in the late 1980s, America's productivity began a downward trend and could no longer keep pace with industrialized nations such as Japan and Korea. For example, Japanese automobile manufacturers require an average of approximately 15 hours to produce one new car. U.S. manufacturers require an average of 20 hours. When American automobile manufacturers must pay their unionized workforce higher wages and better benefits than their Japanese and Korean competitors, taking longer to produce a car puts the American companies at a competitive disadvantage.

By the time the first crop of Me-Geners became adults, they had grown accustomed to being taken care of by their over-indulgent parents. Consequently, these Me-Geners faced a dilemma: Who would take care of them now? The obvious answer was a ready-and-willing federal government. Adult Me-Geners began to view the government in the same way they had always viewed their parents—as an omnipresent provider to indulge their appetites and rescue them from their own irresponsibility.

As Me-Geners came of voting age, there were plenty of pandering politicians willing to indulge the entitlement mentality of this new voting bloc, and none more skillfully than President Obama. Many of these politicians who use the public's money to buy voter loyalty and encourage voter dependency are liberals, but not all. Too many so-called conservatives have been just as quick to use the promise of government largesse to ensure their own re-elections.

Some Work Ethic Basics

The work ethic is what individuals and societies believe about work as a concept. These beliefs translate into their attitudes toward work. Is work good or bad? Is it delight or drudgery? Is it a blessing or a curse? Should work be done only by lesser members of society or should all people work? Is work something to be actively sought or assiduously avoided? How people answer these questions is determined by their work ethic.

Throughout history, the views of individuals and societies concerning work have evolved. Ancient Hebrews thought of work as drudgery inflicted on them as punishment for the disobedience of Adam and Eve in the Garden of Eden. Ancient Greeks also viewed work with a jaundiced eye. They saw it as something to be done by slaves, not by gentlemen. Philosophers such as Plato and Aristotle thought work interfered with the more important human endeavors such as music, philosophy, art, and literature. Romans, like the Greeks, thought of work as the domain of slaves; something they should avoid so as not to blur the line between master and minion.

During the Middle-Ages, attitudes toward work began to change, but only slightly. Instead of being viewed as something to be avoided, work took on a utilitarian aspect. Work was still viewed as lacking any intrinsic value, but it did become an accepted way of providing for a family and avoiding the need for charity. In other words, work was now perceived as having value but only in the sense that it allowed man to independently provide for his daily bread. It still had no *intrinsic* value.

It was during the Protestant Reformation that the work-as-drudgery attitude of people began to change. Martin Luther and John Calvin contributed more than anyone to the new perspective on work that is now directly associated with the Protestant Reformation. As a result of the teachings of Luther and Calvin, Christian-dominated societies began to view work as being God-ordained for the glory of God and the fulfillment of God's purpose on earth. This, in turn, made it inherently good. A logical extension of this new perspective was to view working diligently as a way to serve and honor God as well as a way to thank Him for the opportunity work provided to improve one's circumstances. This thankful, diligent attitude toward work crystallized into what eventually became known as the *Protestant work ethic,* although the first use of the term did not occur until much later.

The term "Protestant work ethic" was coined by German economist and sociologist, Max Weber, in his landmark book, *The Protestant Ethic and the Spirit of Capitalism* (1904 and 1905). Weber attributed the advanced development, quality of life, and prosperity enjoyed by western society to the positive work ethic of Christians. The concept has also been called the Puritan work ethic by those who associate it with John Calvin's emphasis on hard work as a Christian obligation and as evidence of salvation. Calvin professed that those who are saved will show evidence of that fact through, among other things, their dedication to thrift, diligence, self-discipline, self-reliance, responsibility, accountability, delayed gratification, and hard work. This is the concept that came to be known variably as the Protestant or the Puritan work ethic.

Work Ethic Defined

To understand the American version of the work ethic, it is necessary to first understand the Protestant work ethic as envisioned by Calvin. The Protestant work ethic that grew out of the teachings of Calvin can be summarized as follows:

> God has blessed Christians with opportunities to improve their lives through hard work and He has decreed that work is good. Therefore, Christians have a duty to honor and serve God through thrift, diligence, self-reliance, self-discipline, responsibility, accountability, deferred gratification, and hard work. Approaching work in this way is a sign of one's salvation. For Christians, to approach work in a thankful and diligent manner is to follow the Word and will of God.

American Work Ethic

The American work ethic is a direct descendant of the Protestant work ethic. It is a peculiarly American mix of Christian values, rugged individualism, entrepreneurship, economic necessity, patriotism, and the need to compete in order to get ahead. This multifaceted version of the work ethic can be summarized as follows:

> Work is good because it: 1) provides individuals with opportunities to achieve financial security, professional success, personal satisfaction, and material wealth; 2) affords individuals opportunities to contribute to society; 3) helps entrepreneurs who create jobs achieve maximum competitiveness through peak performance and continual improvement, and 4) helps America maintain its freedom and position of leadership in the world. Consequently, people should approach work with an attitude of thrift, diligence, self-reliance, self-discipline, responsibility, accountability, and deferred gratification. Further, people should take pride in working hard and in doing a good job no matter what their job may be.

The Protestant work ethic played a critical role in the development of the American colonies and the establishment of the United States. In fact, one of our founding fathers—Benjamin Franklin—became the unofficial spokesman for the work ethic by recording his thoughts on the subject in his publication, *Poor Richard's Almanac* (although historians now agree that Franklin did not always take his own advice). As our nation grew, the work ethic played a critical role in the achievement of manifest destiny and the eventual establishment of America as an economic superpower.

America is the last great bastion of freedom in the world, but it is also a nation whose freedom is threatened from within by a growing entitlement mentality that is fast replacing the entrepreneurial spirit and traditional work ethic. America's ability to maintain its position of leadership in the world is dependent on the ability of individual Americans and businesses to out-think, out-work, and out-perform the competition in the global arena. Outperforming global competition at the individual and organizational levels requires an entrepreneurial spirit and positive work ethic.

Why the Work Ethic is So Important in Today's Global World

A nation's quality of life in the age of globalization is determined in large measure by the competitiveness of its private sector. The competitiveness of the private sector is determined by many factors, but none more than the performance of individual businesses. The performance of a business, in turn, is largely a function of the performance of its personnel, and few things affect the performance of people more than their work ethic. Of course, knowledge and skills are critical elements of human performance, but unless they are energized by a positive work ethic, knowledge and skills are just idle assets. Sarah Palin will need to drive this point home continually during her campaign for the presidency.

Noah Webster was referring to this fact when he said: "The virtues of men are of more consequence to society than their abilities; and for this reason, the heart should be cultivated with more assiduity than the head."[5] A nation's work ethic is a major determinant of its ability to compete in the global marketplace. Correspondingly, a nation's ability to compete in the global marketplace is a major determinant of its quality of life. It follows from this that a declining work ethic will result in a declining quality of life. This is the situation that now confronts America. Rather than encouraging entrepreneurship, individual initiative, and self-reliance, the government is adopting socialist policies that: 1) penalize those at all levels who have a good work ethic; 2)provide bailouts, handouts, and entitlements; and 3) result in burdensome regulations and oppressive centralized controls.

Ultimate Consequences of Socialism and Entitlement in America

Unfortunately a declining quality of life is not the worst of what Americans face in the 21st century if capitalism, the entrepreneurial spirit, and the work ethic are not restored. The even greater threat is to our freedom and liberty. In a world where the hate-America-crowd is growing steadily in both influence and power, our ability to maintain economic, military, and moral superiority has never been more critical or more at risk. America's ability to retain its historical position of global leadership is a function of numerous intertwined and mutually-dependent factors, one of the more important of which is our nation's work ethic.

In today's hyper-competitive global marketplace, consistent peak performance and continual improvement of performance are organizational imperatives for commercial enterprises. Consequently, more than ever, employers need to have an entrepreneurial spirit and need their personnel to have a positive work ethic. In fact, only by restoring the work ethic can America hope to regain the market losses it has incurred over the last three decades to Japan, Korea, India, and China in some of our most critical commercial sectors.

As commercial enterprises in other industrialized nations continue to whittle away at the markets of American companies, the quality of life in the United States is gradually eroding and the freedoms we have historically enjoyed are increasingly at risk. Whereas the United States historically maintained its quality of life through unrivaled productivity, we are now depending on out-of-control borrowing. The United States is like a family, once well-off, that is now forced to use credit cards to maintain its standard of living. Such an approach can lead only to insolvency, and sooner rather than later.

The relationship between a nation's entrepreneurial spirit and work ethic and its freedom and liberty is clear and compelling. The less competitive a nation, the more debt it is forced to incur. The more debt a nation incurs, the more it becomes a slave to lender nations. America is rapidly becoming a slave. This situation is bad enough in and of itself. But what makes it even worse is that the nations that lend the most money to the United States are not respecters of freedom and liberty, nor do they have the best interests of America at heart. Moreover, the military might that is essential to protect America against its enemies depends on our nation's wealth and technological superiority. Socialism will eventually destroy that wealth and technological superiority. This is why rejecting socialism and restoring capitalism, the entrepreneurial spirit, and the traditional work ethic in America are such important commitments.

The Surprising Truth Concerning What Americans Think About Socialism

In a nation that built the strongest economy in the history of the world on the basis of capitalism, entrepreneurship, and a positive work ethic, one would think socialism would be anathema. Unfortunately, this is not the case. In a poll released by Scott Rasmussen, respondents were asked the following question: "Which is a better system—capitalism or socialism? Those who chose capitalism were in the majority, but just barely (53 percent).[6] This means that in America—the land of freedom and opportunity—47 percent of our citizens either prefer socialism or do not know which system they prefer. Either way, this is a disturbing result. This 47 percent represents a critical constituency for Sarah Palin in the next presidential election. This population cohort is still malleable enough to turn to capitalism if a presidential candidate can make the case for doing so. Sarah Palin, by her example, words, and commitment can be that candidate.

Perhaps the most disturbing aspect of the Rasmussen poll is how divided adults under thirty years of age were over the question of socialism versus capitalism. In other words, the Me-Generation cannot be depended on to preserve the worldview and economic system that made America the most powerful nation in the world. Many Me-Geners actually prefer a system that has a long and consistent record of failure—socialism. According to the Rasmussen poll, adults under the age of thirty responded to the question as follows: 37 percent prefer capitalism, 33 percent prefer socialism, and 30 percent are undecided.[7] This is an indictment of America's education system, mass media, and much of the church. It is something all Americans must come together to remedy.

Eberle summarizes his thoughts on America's turn toward socialism as follows: "We are at a crossroads, and we must fight to get America back on track. The American way is not an easy way. No one ever said it was. It's not about what the government can give you. The government can't give a person anything it does not first take away from someone else. No person is entitled to what another person earns. The American way is about respecting the rights of the individual and promoting an economic and political system that provides opportunity for all."[8]

Sarah Palin's Role in Restoring Capitalism, Entrepreneurship, and the Work Ethic

As a presidential candidate in the next election, Sarah Palin will command the attention of all Americans. This will give her an opportunity to make the case for restoring capitalism, the entrepreneurial spirit, and the traditional work ethic; to speak to the hearts of those Americans who are concerned about the damage President Obama's socialist programs have done to America's economy and to the freedom and liberty of the American public.

It will also give her an opportunity to educate those who are riding in the economic wagon concerning the damage they are doing to themselves and their country. Her challenge will be to show Americans who have developed an entitlement mentality why the values of thrift, diligence, self-reliance, self-discipline, responsibility, accountability, deferred gratification, and hard work will serve them and all Americans better in the long run than will an entitlement mentality and a dependence on government.

NOTES

1. Walter Williams, "Congress is to blame and should be held accountable," Syndicated column in the *Northwest Florida Daily News,* October 12, 2008.

2. *Ibid.*

3. Walter Williams, "America's immorality will bring this nation down," Syndicated column in the *Northwest Florida Daily News,* April 2, 2009.

4. Congressman Tom Price, "Federal bailout of auto industry," *The American Legion,* April 2009, 10.

5. Founder's Quote Daily, *The Patriot Post.* Retrieved from http://patriotpost.us, December 16, 2008.

6. Bobby Eberle, "Socialism vs. Capitalism...And the Winner is..." *The Loft.* Retrieved from http://www.gopusa.com/theloft/?p=1272.

7. *Ibid.*

8. *Ibid.*

Four

BE FORTHRIGHT

"America's Christian history is a fact. It is not honest to redefine history or tamper with the historical record just so that people of differing opinions are not offended. It was America's moral choice that made this nation the envy of the world and a haven for the oppressed."

—Gary DeMar
America's Christian History: The Untold Story

Barack Obama appears determined to spend his years in office insulting Christians and catering to Muslims. In 2009, he denied that America is a Christian nation and asserted that the United States is one of the largest Muslim nations in the world—he was wrong on both accounts. Also in 2009, when he refused to participate in the National Day of Prayer but was the keynote speaker at a major Muslim celebration, President Obama insulted Christians of all denominations. His obvious preference for Islam has hurt him in the eyes of a substantial portion of the American public, including many people who claim no religion.

Although the number has declined somewhat over the years, more than 70 percent of Americans still profess to be Christians. This fact gives Sarah Palin an opportunity to stand up for millions of Americans who are concerned about what President Obama's absurd denials of our nation's Christian heritage may really mean. Sarah Palin is open and forthright about her religion and refreshingly willing to evangelize by example. In other words, religion is a way of life for Sarah Palin, rather than a way to get elected. She is not one of those pseudo-Christians who gets religion in the months leading up to an election and forgets about it as soon as the campaign is over.

Because she has credibility when it comes to religion, Sarah Palin can do something that will be critically important in the next election: be forthright about the failings of secular humanism—the unofficial religion of the left—and unapologetic about America's Christian heritage. Even Americans who claim no religion know that President Obama's obvious preference for the Muslim religion is potentially explosive in a nation that is still overwhelmingly Christian in its leanings. The majority of Americans will be reassured by a presidential candidate who quietly lives the kind of life prescribed by Christ and is not afraid to acknowledge our country's Christian roots. That candidate can be Sarah Palin.

Secular Humanism: The Religion of the Left

One of the most disingenuous arguments of the left is that religion should be kept out of the public lives of American citizens. Freedom FROM religion is a fundamental tenet of secular humanism. The left's interpretation of the First Amendment is that it requires a forced separation of religion from all aspects of public life. This is a blatantly disingenuous and hypocritical interpretation of the Constitution. The disingenuous aspect is that the left knowingly and purposefully misinterpret the "establishment" and "free exercise" clauses of the First Amendment which say: "Congress shall make no law respecting an establishment of religion, or prohibiting the free exercise thereof." Beyond choosing to ignore the historical fact that the founders intended this language to protect against the type of national state-supported church they had fled England to avoid, their interpretation is disingenuous because it focuses on the first clause and ignores the second.

The hypocritical aspect of the left's interpretation of the First Amendment is that they are not opposed to religion per se, just the Christian religion. In fact, they typically bend over backwards to accommodate Islam, Hinduism, and Buddhism and any religion other than Christianity. Further, secular humanists are just as religious as Christians; the difference is found in whom and what they worship. While Christians worship the God of the Holy Bible, secular humanists worship a limited and ever-changing god: man. The religion of the left is secular humanism. This is a point that must be made evident during the next presidential campaign.

Two Religions with
Different Starting Points

Consider what happens when two people try to settle an issue of right and wrong, but lack a common basis for deciding. They are like two surveyors trying to settle a property claim who begin their work from two different starting points. The claim will never be settled. The only way one survey can validate or refute the other is if the surveyors start at a common point. The lesson in this analogy is one that secular humanists choose to ignore. Those who do not wish to be bound by the moral constraints of Christianity must find an alternative. That alternative, at least for the left, is secular humanism. While Christians base their system of ethics on the Ten Commandments and the Word of God, secular humanists base theirs on the concept of moral relativism. Christianity and secular humanism are both religions—with completely opposite ethical starting points.

Moral Relativism Defined

Moral relativism is a fundamental tenet of the secular humanist's worldview. It claims that right and wrong are culturally-based and defined by the needs of man, thus they are subject to the determination of the individual. If man is god, as is the case with moral relativism, then man decides right and wrong. In layman's terms, moral relativism means that there are no absolutes; individuals decide for themselves what is right and what is wrong—both are relative. This is convenient for those who wish to avoid confrontations with others over questions of right and wrong, but it quickly breaks down when what one individual thinks is right conflicts with what another individual thinks.

Secular humanists believe in the evolutionary view that life on earth is the result of countless cosmic accidents. This being the case, life is accidental and therefore lacks any meaning more substantive than whatever makes any given individual happy at any given moment. Consequently, anything the individual chooses to do is acceptable because, in the long run, it is not going to matter anyway. From the convenient perspective of moral relativism, if something is right for me, it is right period; an enticing point of view for those who feel constrained by the Judeo-Christian ethic and do not want to think about the logical and practical consequences of their own beliefs. In adopting moral relativism, secular humanists are applying a strategy that is as old as mankind itself: if the rules get in the way of what you want, make new rules.

Opinion polls show that Americans are tiring of moral relativism and the deleterious effect it is having on society. Many Americans are beginning to notice that every time they pick up their morning newspaper or watch the nightly news they are confronted by ever-worsening examples of man's inhumanity to man. School shootings, murders at work, road rage, abortion, rape, divorce, children born to children, out-of-wedlock babies, R-rated television for children, single-parent families, gang violence, drugs, pornography, child abuse, abominable language, criminals running the prisons, failure of judges to punish criminals, and the list goes on. These and other examples of the coarsening of American society are the result of moral relativism, the ethical corollary to secular humanism.

The left likes to portray moral relativism as a neutral concept, but it is obviously not neutral, for it is hostile to morality. The results of this abominable concept are anything but neutral—in fact, just the opposite. The on-going degradation of society from the effects of moral relativism disturbs and frightens many Americans. It is why so many are crying out for a presidential candidate with the courage to confront secular humanists and hold them responsible for the cultural ravages of moral relativism. Americans are ready for a presidential candidate who is willing to hold the left accountable for the results of the moral decay that is self-evident in society. Because she has a long and consistent record of living according to her quietly professed beliefs, Sarah Palin has the credibility to confront advocates of secular humanism and moral relativism, detail the logical and practical consequences of their false ideas, and hold them accountable for what their beliefs have wrought.

Is Moral Relativism Morally Neutral?

Secular humanists like to claim that moral relativism—you do your thing and I'll do mine—is a morally neutral concept. This, of course, is a practical impossibility—nothing is morally neutral. In an article entitled, "Moral Relativism – Neutral Thinking," the president of Planned Parenthood is quoted as saying: "[T]eaching morality doesn't mean imposing my moral values on others. It means sharing wisdom, giving reasons for believing as I do – and then trusting others to think and judge for themselves."[1] Even a cursory reading of this statement reveals the absurdity of its claim—the claim of moral neutrality. The only reason for making such a statement is to influence the thinking of others. Hence, the arguments for moral relativism are, by their very nature, self-refuting.

Secular humanists who argue for moral relativism argue against themselves. For example, tell a proponent of moral relativism that you advocate child abuse and you are likely to be reported to government authorities. However, if the secular humanist who reports you really believes that right and wrong are matters of individual choice, how can he argue against child abuse? After all, there are certainly individuals—unfortunately many of them—who make the choice to abuse children. If these individuals are secular humanists and they believe their heinous behavior is right, then—according to the definition of moral relativism—it is right.

Because of this inherent flaw in their philosophy, secular humanists have taken to adding a disclaimer to their arguments for moral relativism. They now say that whatever the individual believes to be right is right *unless it hurts someone else*. But, of course, the disclaimer is as flawed as the concept. If everything is relative, how can it be wrong to hurt someone else? If it is wrong to hurt someone else, why do secular humanists do it? For example, why do they advocate abortion on demand? Such a practice—by the secular humanist's own definition—must be wrong. After all, it certainly hurts the children who are aborted, the mothers involved, and society in general. There is no end to these types of dilemmas, and no acceptable answer to them from proponents of moral relativism. Logic is not on the side of secular humanists.

Obviously, moral relativism is a flawed concept. Nevertheless, it is considered sacred ground among members of the left. For example, a Zogby poll shows that 75 percent of college professors teach that there is no such thing as right and wrong; that good and evil are relative concepts based on individual preferences and cultural interpretation.[2] Yet, these same professors are quick to claim that Christian and conservative worldviews are wrong, or worse. Consider what Robert Brandon, professor of biology and philosophy at Duke University, had to say when questioned about liberal bias at his institution: "If, as John Stuart Mill said, stupid people are generally conservative, then there are lots of conservatives we will never hire... Members of academia tend to be a bit smarter than average."[3] Apparently they are also a bit more arrogant.

William McGuffey, the author of the classic elementary readers used to teach generations of Americans, said this: "Erase all thought and fear of God from a community, and selfishness and sensuality will absorb the whole man."[4] This is a prophetic statement because it provides an accurate description of what is happening in American society due to secular humanism and moral relativism. Moreover, moral relativism is, as the framers and ratifiers of the Constitution knew, incompatible with freedom. If everything is relative and there is no right or wrong, then there is nothing wrong with civil government officials using the power of government to rule tyrannically. Moral relativism was fundamental to the 20th century's totalitarian governments and the brutal horrors of their misrule. This is the message that Sarah Palin must convey to the American public in the next election.

Humanist Manifesto: **The Bible for Secular Humanists/Moral Relativists**

Like most religions, secular humanism has a "bible." Liberals look to the Humanist *Manifesto* as their sacred book. There are actually three versions of the *Manifesto*: 1) the original Humanist *Manifesto* published in 1933 (*Humanist Manifesto I*), 2) *Humanist Manifesto II* published in 1973, and 3) *Humanism and Its Aspirations* published in 2003 (*Humanist Manifesto III*). All three of these documents describe a worldview absent of God or any other kind of higher power. The god of humanism is man. All three versions of the *Manifesto* have been signed by prominent liberals, but not without some controversy among those on the left.

The *Manifesto* has been updated and revised over time as humanist thinking has evolved and as disagreements among its proponents have emerged. This shows a fundamental weakness of secular humanism—the fickle nature of its god: man. The fact that it is man-centered is just one of many factors that undermine the validity of secular humanism as a religion. In response to the evolution of humanist thinking, each successive version of the *Manifesto* has sought to correct the perceived weaknesses of its predecessor and answer criticisms from both the right and left.

Humanist Manifesto I

The original *Manifesto* was written in 1933. It presented a new belief system to replace religions founded on supernatural revelation. The new belief system it proposed amounted to an egalitarian worldview based on voluntary mutual cooperation among all people; an ideal rendered impossible from the outset by the sinful nature of man. There was disagreement about various aspects of the *Manifesto* among those who developed it; a predictable circumstance inherent in all human endeavors. Consequently, the originally proposed title, *"The Humanist Manifesto,"* had to be changed to *"A Humanist Manifesto."*

Prophetically, the original *Manifesto* contained a basic tenet that now haunts, embarrasses, and even angers modern-day liberals. It referred to humanism as a religion; something today's liberals go to great lengths to deny since freedom FROM religion is the cornerstone of their man-centered worldview. If secular humanists must admit that their views of morality are a religion, their efforts to ban religion from the marketplace of ideas are exposed for what they really are—hypocrisy. If this happens, the left will be forced to admit that Christianity is their real target, not religion; something even a casual observer of American culture already knows.

Humanist Manifesto II

The atrocities of World War II perpetrated by the followers of Hitler, Tojo, and Stalin—all moral relativists—revealed the shortcomings of the basic premise of the original *Manifesto*. With the evidence of Hitler's death camps, Stalin's pogroms, and Tojo's rape of Nanking revealed to the world, even the most idealistic of humanists had to admit that their hope for a worldwide egalitarian society based on voluntary mutual cooperation might have been too optimistic. One can only wonder why the horrors of World War II did not lead humanists to abandon their belief in moral relativism entirely.

Admitting the naiveté of the first document, drafters of the second *Manifesto* took a more realistic approach. Rather than pursuing a worldwide egalitarian society based on voluntary mutual cooperation, the drafters of *Manifesto II* set what they called "more realistic" goals, including the elimination of war and poverty. Of course, if intellectual and moral relativism were valid concepts, there would be nothing wrong with war and no reason to eliminate poverty. None of the document's authors or supporters thought to ask how these goals could be achieved without changing the heart of man. Such it is and has always been with the left. Since man is god, why try to change his heart? When one will not admit that man has a sinful nature, it becomes much easier to believe that war and hunger can be eliminated by simply displaying heart-tugging bumper stickers on the back of your car. After all, slogans such as "Give Peace a Chance"—if displayed on enough bumpers—will surely end war.

One of the more controversial and frequently quoted verses from *Manifesto II* is: "We are responsible for what we are and what we will be... No deity will save us; we must save ourselves."[5] Another verse, one that clearly reveals a fundamental goal of the left is: "[T]he battleground for humankind's future must be waged and won in the public school classroom by teachers who correctly perceive their role as the proselytizers of a new faith: a religion of humanity that recognizes and respects the spark of what theologians call divinity in every human being...Utilizing a classroom instead of a pulpit to convey humanist values in whatever subject they teach, regardless of the educational level – preschool day care or large state university."[6] As a graduate student many years ago, I (David Goetsch) obtained a copy of the *Manifesto* and underscored these lines. Then when liberal professors espoused their views on separating church and state and keeping religion out of the classroom, I would raise my hand and quote the *Manifesto*. It goes without saying that I was not a popular student in these classes.

As is always the case in the endeavors of man, there was much disagreement in the liberal community about various aspects of *Manifesto II*. Consequently, only a few ardent proponents agreed to sign the document when it was first released. To solve this problem, the *Manifesto* has since been widely circulated with a caveat making it clear that it is not necessary to agree with every detail of the document in order to be a signatory. This disingenuous disclaimer had the intended effect, and the document eventually garnered more signatures.

Humanist Manifesto III

The latest version of the *Manifesto—Humanist Manifesto III*—is titled, *Humanism and Its Aspirations*. It was published by the American Humanist Association in 2003. This version of the *Manifesto* is purposefully shorter than its predecessors. It presents six broad beliefs that encompass the humanist philosophy as professed by the American Humanist Association but that leave plenty of room for interpretation, this latter characteristic being necessary to avoid much of the disagreement within humanist circles that surrounded the two early versions of the *Manifesto*—and to garner more support. These six broad statements of belief may be summarized as follows:

- Knowledge of the world is empirically derived

(by observation, experimentation, and rational analysis).

- Unguided evolutionary change has the result of making humans integral to nature.

- Ethical values are established by humans and are based on human need that has been tested by experience.

- Humans are fulfilled in life by participating in the service of humane ideals.

- Humans are, by nature, social beings. Therefore, they find meaning in relationships.

- Humans maximize their happiness by working to benefit society[7]

These six statements are so laden with problems that we could easily devote an entire chapter to critiquing them, but doing so is beyond our purpose here. Although these six statements of belief are not as specific as those contained in the earlier versions of the *Manifesto*, they still support the same worldview. For example, the first statement—the humanist belief in empiricism—rules out God's special revelation as set forth in the Bible and reveals an astounding ignorance of the philosophical problems inherent in man-centered empiricism. The second statement is a reiteration of the humanist belief in Darwinian evolution which, of course, is the basis for the American Humanist Association's on-going attacks on creationism, as well as its justification for supporting abortion.

The third statement makes clear that the Bible has no place in establishing right and wrong. Rather, what is right or wrong depends on human need. Who decides what is right and wrong when human needs differ—as they always do—is an open question with secular humanists, as well as a fundamental weakness in their belief system. The last three statements make it clear that humanists reject God, the Bible, and what is usually called religion.

In the fourth statement, fulfillment comes from the service of humane ideals, not service to God and His Kingdom. Christians also believe in service, but they know that service to man comes from Christ's admonition to love your neighbor as yourself. They also know that God's word and law, not man's desires, define human ideals; they know that the "tender mercies" of the wicked are cruel. In the fifth statement, human relationships are presented as the ultimate goal, as opposed to a relationship with God. Finally, humanists believe that service to society is the ultimate service because, for them, man is god. Christians also believe in service to society, but as a way to serve the God who created man and to follow Christ's admonition to love your neighbor as yourself.

Manifesto III is shorter and more to the point than its predecessors, and its six statements of belief are less specific, but its rejection of God is just as much a cornerstone as it was in the early versions. The wording and length of the various versions of the *Manifesto* have changed over time, but its basic man-as-god philosophy has not. Herein is found the never-changing source of the unbridgeable gulf between secular humanism and Christianity, as well as the source of the left's religious bigotry toward Christianity.

Secular humanists apparently believe they can peace-fully co-exist with religions other than Christianity—hence their accommodation of Islam, Hinduism, and Bud-dhism. Of course, they are only fooling themselves. There is a philosophical train wreck coming farther down the track involving secular humanists and Islam, but for now the left has focused its animosity on Christianity because they know that if Christianity is right, they are wrong. This simple fact frightens secular humanists so much that they feel compelled to belittle, attack, and even suppress the Christian worldview in the classroom, the public square, the marketplace of ideas and anywhere else it might rear its unwelcome head.

Using Higher Education to Promote Moral Relativism

With the help of the American Civil Liberties Union (ACLU) and the National Education Association (NEA), secular humanists have made much progress in turning America's public schools into indoctrination camps for the left. Now that they can claim victory in America's public elementary and high schools, secular humanists are hard at work pursuing the same agenda in higher education. Because colleges and universities are mag-nets for secular humanists who believe in moral rela-tivism, progress in turning institutions of higher edu-cation into indoctrination camps for the left has been swift and effective.

Since their god is man, it was necessary for secular

humanists to establish an ethical corollary to humanism that would render any standards of absolute right and wrong obsolete. "During much of early American history, moral education in colleges and universities moved from being grounded in appeals to special revelation to universal appeals to human nature, natural law, or reason. In other words, teachers and textbook writers attempted to locate moral agreement in something common to all humanity."[8] Thus was born the concept of moral relativism.

Another glaring flaw is that one thing that is common to all humanity is moral *disagreement*, not moral agreement. Moral disagreement divides people. It does not and cannot unite them. Moral relativism cannot unite men who hold different moral views. Nor can it unite people who, holding to moral relativism, seek absolute power over others by any means.

The fundamental flaw of moral relativism is that the only things common to all of humanity are its creation by God and its sinful nature, neither of which secular humanists will accept.   When your god is man—with all of his inherent moral frailties—moral relativism is the best you can do in the way of an ethical framework.

In order for secular humanism to prevail in American society, it is necessary for its proponents to control or at least influence the institutions that weave the tapestry of its moral and social conventions. This is why the left is so intent on dominating institutions of higher education. Anne Colby, writing for the *Journal of College and Character*, had this to say about why the domination of colleges and universities is so important:

Of course, many kinds of social institutions have important roles to play in educating citizens. Religious organizations and other voluntary associations, the media, and education at the elementary and secondary levels are among the most important of these. But higher education is critical, because universities and colleges are the institutions most clearly charged with leading the development of new and deeper understanding through research and scholarship and preparing new generations by teaching not only information and skills, but their significance for creating the future, both personally and collectively. Higher education has tremendous opportunities for being a positive force in society as it reaches an ever larger segment of the population, including virtually all leaders in both government and the private sector. It is a powerful influence in shaping individual's relationships with each other and their communities, and we need to take steps to ensure its influence is constructive rather than corrosive. [9]

This statement clearly articulates what secular humanists well know: he who controls higher education in America controls America's future. Herein is found the left's need to suppress the moral absolutes of Christianity and replace them with the ever-changing whims of moral relativism. Herein also is found the means by which the left has done this and is doing it.

Values-Neutrality and Christianity in Higher Education

One of the arguments frequently heard from moral relativists to justify suppressing biblical views on campus is that higher education should be *values-neutral,* an absurd argument made to appeal to young people who have not learned to think critically. Those who make this argument claim that values should be addressed by the family and church rather than institutions of higher education. While Christians will certainly agree that families and churches should play the key role in establishing values in individuals, there are several problems with this argument. The most fundamental being is that it represents a practical impossibility.

Even if university faculties tried to be values-neutral, they could not possibly achieve such a goal. Every human being has a worldview that is based on his most deeply held convictions. Consequently, every issue, principle, and concept discussed in a university classroom is informed by the worldviews of those involved in the discussion. A liberal professor will see the world through a whole different set of lenses than one who is conservative or Christian. His worldview will shape his perspective concerning the issue in question. Another problem with the argument is the hypocrisy in it. Left-leaning university faculties—rather than attempting to be neutral—invest much time and effort in trying to undermine the values they claim should be left to the development of families and churches.

Colby is correct in saying "closer scrutiny makes it clear that educational institutions cannot be values neutral. For decades educators have recognized the power of the 'hidden curriculum' in schools and the moral messages it carries. The hidden curriculum is the (largely unexamined) practices through which the school and its teachers operate, maintaining discipline, assigning grades and other rewards, and managing their relationships with their students and each other." [10] She continues, "most of life situations are inherently ambiguous, and their moral significance is underdetermined by available facts. In order to find meaning and clarity amid this ambiguity, people develop habits of moral interpretation and intuition through which they perceive the world." [11] In other words, they have a worldview that determines how they interpret everything they observe, read, hear, and experience.

Liberal professors understand that "people develop habits of moral interpretation and intuition through which they perceive the world." They merely want to control this development. This is why they are so determined to replace the Christian and conservative worldviews with one that embraces moral relativism. Liberal professors who operate on the basis of the presuppositions of secular humanism, and maintain only adversarial relationships with Christian and conservative students are being anything but values-neutral. Further, they do not want their students to be values neutral. They want students to reject the values they brought to college and embrace those of the left.

The Left's Struggle with the Consequences of Moral Relativism

Secular humanists, with their devotion to moral relativism, are continually sticking their heads in an intellectual vise, one jaw of which is formed by their professed beliefs and the other by the consequences of those beliefs. Secular-humanists cling tenaciously to the non-absolutes of moral relativism, while on the other hand deploring their consequences. Those consequences include: cheating, dishonesty, irresponsibility, a general lack of respect, violence, drug abuse, and intolerance of diversity—racial, cultural, religious, moral, and intellectual.

If morality is relative and self-determined, then cheating is wrong only if one gets caught because honesty has value only to the extent that it serves one's purpose at the moment. If morality is relative, then an individual's only responsibility is to his own personal needs or desires at any given point in time. Interestingly, liberal professors do not want their own relativistic beliefs practiced in their classes. Further, it is apparent that young people—no matter what their worldviews may be—do not learn to respect each other by observing their Christian and conservative peers being treated disrespectfully by left-wing secular humanists.

When there is only one point of view allowed in a discussion, is it any wonder that young people fail to develop critical-thinking skills, a universal problem in America? Finally, secular humanists cannot possibly teach tolerance of diversity by being openly intolerant of it. These are the conundrums that secular humanists inflict on themselves by advocating moral relativism while suppressing Christian and conservative views, and these are the conundrums that Sarah Palin must point out to the American public in the next presidential campaign.

The Case Against Moral Relativism

To unthinking proponents of moral relativism, one of its more appealing aspects is that it appears to preclude the need for discussion, debate, or disagreement. There are plenty of people who just want to be left alone to do their own thing. The apparent ethical indifference of moral relativism appeals to such people. The last thing they want is the hassle of dealing with issues of right and wrong. Moral relativism allows these head-in-the-sand types to avoid conflict by simply adopting a *you-do-your-thing-and-I-will-do-mine* attitude toward the world.

Moral relativism gives it proponents a basis for rationalizing doing whatever they want to do. It is the perfect philosophy for people who do not wish to have their behavior constrained or their lifestyle inhibited by inconvenient rules. This appeal of moral relativism is why author Ryan Dobson calls it "sin in a toga," by which he means that it is nothing more than "selfishness and hedonism and rebellion dressed up in philosopher's robes."[12] In his book, *Be Intolerant Becuase Some Things Are Just Stupid,* Dobson says: "Moral relativism is not a philosophy you would arrive at by studying the world around you. If you put something under your microscope or do real science with your chemistry set or point your telescope at the stars, you will not arrive at the conclusion that there are no constants in the universe. The only way to come up with moral relativism is to begin with an agenda and then look for ways to make your agenda possible. Your starting point is not an observation of the universe, but an action you want to take."[13] This is an important point because one of the foundational tenets of secular humanism is empiricism: the belief that knowledge of the world is gained through observation, experimentation, and rational analysis as opposed to biblical revelation. In reality, empiricism refutes moral relativism.

Dobson gives several reasons why moral relativism is what he calls a "broken philosophy:"[14]

- Moral relativism is empty, meaningless, and purposeless. It can provide permission to do what should not be done or to tolerate what should not be tolerated, but it cannot provide hope. Nor can it give its proponents peace or answers to life's quandaries, problems, or mysteries.

- Moral relativism is self-refuting. The idea that there is no absolute truth—the cornerstone of moral relativism—is itself a declaration of absolute truth.

- People cling to moral relativism in the same way and for the same reason that smokers continue to smoke: they want what it does for them more than they want the benefits of quitting. [15]

Moral relativism is also a philosophy that breaks or deeply injures society. For moral relativism, far from leading to a "live and let live" attitude in society, leads logically in two directions: 1) anarchic lawlessness, and 2) totalitarian tyranny. If moral relativism is true and there are no absolute principles which define right and wrong or good and evil, then there is nothing wrong with anyone doing whatever he feels like doing. If moral relativism is true, then rape, child abuse, murder, and other heinous crimes are not wrong. If moral relativism is true, then justice is a myth and no law should restrain individual action or choices. This is known as "anarchy." If moral relativism is true, there are no moral laws or principles to limit the action of rulers. Rulers are therefore free to use force and deceit to do whatever they want. This belief, of course, opens the door to tyranny and totalitarianism.

Secular humanism is the religion of the left. It has its own bible: the *Humanist Manifesto*; its own ethical construct: moral relativism; and its own god: man. This is not simply a clever ruse on the part of Christians to render the anti-religion views of secular humanism null and void. The *Humanist Manifesto* makes clear that secular humanism is a religion developed specifically to replace those religions of the world that are based on supernatural revelation. The facts are clear. Secular humanists do not oppose religion, just Christianity. There is a name for this type of bias. It is called religious bigotry.

Rejecting Secular Humanism and Moral Relativism in the Next Election

The effects of secular humanism and moral relativism on American society are beyond dispute. Man's inhumanity to man assaults Americans at every turn. As a society, we are awash in the effects of moral relativism: violence, drugs, pornography, abortion, child abuse, promiscuity, road rage, public crudeness, and a general coarsening of society. This downward socio-cultural spiral only accelerated with the election of Barack Obama. Americans are fed up with and frightened by the moral decay they see all around them and are ready to say "no more." What they need is a presidential candidate who is willing to take up the cause and point out the failings of secular humanism and moral relativism. The candidate with the credibility to do this most convincingly is Sarah Palin.

Affirming America's Christian Heritage in the Next Election

As a candidate who is already known as a Christian conservative, Sarah Palin is ideally situated to confront secular humanism and moral relativism with an affirmation of America's Christian heritage. America was founded by Christians—not by 17th and 18th century secular humanists. The moral values of early Americans were based on the Bible and the Christian version of natural law—with some elements of classical ethics—not on the presuppositions of secular humanism. The statesmen who gave us the Declaration of Independence, Articles of Confederation, Constitution, and Bill of Rights were not secular humanists or moral relativists, but overwhelmingly Christians who believed in God-given moral absolutes.

Little wonder then that early American education was distinctly Christian. Early American law, legal thought, and legal education were predominantly Christian. Early state constitutions were, in admittedly varying degrees,

Christian, as were the laws of the states. Such was the social, intellectual, cultural, and political context within which the Constitution and Bill of Rights were produced.

America's Constitution—contrary to the assertions of secular humanists—was a Christian document. It is not silent about God. Rather, it mentions God by clear implication in Article VII's affirmation that the document was developed "in the year of our Lord one thousand seven-hundred eighty-seven." The Constitution is based on a Christian understanding of original sin—that all men, including civil government officials, are adversely affected by sin in every aspect of their being. This is why the Constitution has its carefully-designed, distinctive features. Other Christian ethical and political principles are evident in the original Constitution.

The hostility of secular humanists and moral relativists to Christianity is why they have devoted so much effort to subverting the Constitution and Bill of Rights, and why they try so hard to keep the public ignorant of America's Christian heritage. No political figure is better equipped to take the message of our country's Christian heritage to grassroots Americans than Sarah Palin.

NOTES

1. "Moral Relativism – Neutral Thinking?" Retrieved from http://www.moral-relativism.com on January 21, 2009, 1.

2. Ibid.

3. As quoted in Ben Stein and Phil DeMuth, Can America Survive? (Carlsbad, CA: New Beginnings Press, 2004), 111.

4. "Moral Relativism – Neutral Thinking?" Retrieved from http://www.moral-relativism.com on January 21, 2009, 2.

5. As quoted in "Humanist Manifesto II." Retrieved from http://

en.wikipedia.org/wiki/Humanist_*Manifesto* on January 21, 2009.

6. *Ibid.*

7. *Humanism and Its Aspirations* (American Humanist Association, Washington, D.C., 2003).

8. Perry L. Glanzer and Todd C. Ream, "Educating Different Types of Citizens: Identity, Tradition, Moral Education," *Journal of College & Character,* Vol. IX, No.4, April 2008, 1.

9. Anne Colby, "Whose Values Anyway?" *Journal of College & Character.* Retrieved from http://collegevalues.org/articles.cfm?a=1&id=685, 2.

10. *Ibid*, 3.

11. *Ibid*, 4.

12. Ryan Dobson, *Be Intolerant Because Some Things Are Just Stupid* (Carol Stream, IL: Tyndale House, 2003), 55.

13. *Ibid*, 55-56.

14. *Ibid*, 49.

15. *Ibid*, 50-55.

Five

Do Not Apologize

"Speak softly and carry a big stick."
–Theodore Roosevelt

During the 2008 Presidential campaign, Sarah Palin was criticized by biased media pundits for having no foreign policy experience. The irony in their criticism was that their favored candidate—Barack Obama—was equally lacking in this area, and even more so. He showed this to be the case when, shortly after taking office, he went on what became known as his *worldwide apology tour.* Americans were shocked to turn on the nightly news and hear the President of the United States denouncing his country in front of foreign audiences.

The truth is that most American presidents come into office lacking substantial foreign policy experience. What media pundits do not like to admit is that experience is not even the key issue when it comes to foreign policy. Every president has access to a wealth of talented foreign-policy advisors who can provide the corporate memory, historical background, political perspective, and detailed information the president needs for negotiating and otherwise dealing with our allies and enemies. However, when all is said and done, it is the president's core values, commitment to America's best interests, and moral courage that will determine which advisors will be selected, what advice will be accepted, and how America's foreign policy will be pursued. In this regard, Sarah Palin is much better prepared in the foreign-policy arena than President Obama, a fact that the President's record to date bears out.

President Obama is Popular in Europe for All the Wrong Reasons

In preparing the foreign-policy plank in her campaign platform, Sarah Palin would do well to examine the issue of why President Obama is more popular in Europe than previous American presidents have been. His popularity is not a compliment to his foreign-policy expertise. In fact, just the opposite is true. An objective examination of President Obama's popularity in Europe reveals that it has a disturbing side that should concern Americans.

Shortly after he took office, a poll taken by the Pew Research Center showed that with the election of Barack Obama and the departure of George W. Bush, America's popularity in Europe had increased significantly. Ironically, as the President's approval rating was rising in Europe, it was falling in America. Unfortunately for President Obama, it appears that the joke was on him. Being liked by Europeans is not an asset when so many Americans view Europe as a collection of declining socialist nations whose citizens have over-inflated egos, short memories, and insufficient gratitude.

Worse yet, the President's standing in Europe has proven to be of little value to America because it has failed to produce any tangible foreign-policy benefits. Europeans have not been willing to provide assistance to the United States with Afghanistan, Guantanamo Bay, North Korea, Iran, or any other substantive foreign challenges. This is an important message for Sarah Palin to convey to Americans. She should be prepared to ask President Obama directly: "How has your popularity in Europe helped America?"

There is an old maxim about knowing a person by his enemies. The obverse is also true: you can know a person by his friends. President Obama is scoring few points with Americans by being popular with Europeans. Barack Obama is popular with Europeans because he is philosophically one of them and quick on the draw when apologizing for America. But his supporters are confusing likability with respect. Everyone has known an individual they liked but did not respect.

When it comes to international relations, it would be better for America if our allies and enemies respected President Obama. It would also be better if they knew without a doubt that he would stand firm for the best interests of the United States, whether doing so made him popular or not. Our allies and enemies liking the President matters little, but their respect for him matters greatly. This message should become part of Sarah Palin's campaign rhetoric.

President Obama's Foreign Policy is Characterized by Blunders

President Obama's foreign-policy blunders have given Sarah Palin much ammunition for her campaign and she needs to use it. Many Americans do not trust that President Obama has the best interests of the United States at heart when he interacts with foreign heads of state. The President of the United States wears several hats, all of them important. Arguably, the most important is foreign policy. The occupant of the Oval Office is also supposed to be the leader of the Free World, a fact that has many Americans concerned. President Obama's performance to date in foreign policy bodes poorly for the United States and, in turn, the rest of the Free World. In fact, his performance so far is causing many Americans to question whether President Obama is up to the job of leading the Free World.

Representing the United States in foreign affairs is like playing three-dimensional chess with an ever-changing set of rules. It is a complex game with the highest possible stakes. It demands vision, courage, commitment, stealth, steely nerves, a willingness to take calculated risks, and a thorough understanding of the concept of national interest—ours as well as those of our enemies and allies. Being the leader of the Free World is playing in the big leagues where everyone plays for keeps and there is little room for error. President Obama's performance in foreign affairs has given little indication that he has the best interests of the United States at heart.

Examples such as the following suggest he needed to spend more time in the minor leagues before jumping to the majors. His handling of the Guantanamo issue embarrassed his administration and party. His public statements about North Korea, although on target, had little effect. Unlike the American public, North Korean officials are not swayed by speeches, no matter how well-delivered. After Obama labeled a nuclear-armed North Korea a "grave threat," the communist government thumbed its nose at him by having two American journalists arrested and sentenced to 12 years at hard labor.

The Obama administration was able to eventually secure the release of the two women, but only after the journalists agreed to make groveling apologies to North Korea and President Obama agreed to terms that amounted to buying them out of prison. The journalists were returned to America, which is good. But Americans soon learned that what President Obama gave up to secure their release did nothing to make the world safe from a nuclear North Korea.

Perhaps President Obama's biggest foreign-affairs blunder thus far was his response to election fraud in Iran and to the bigger issue of nuclear proliferation in a country that is the poster child for the hate-America movement. To date, Obama's attempts to reason with the anti-American government of this rogue nation have met with predictable results. Worse yet, President Obama's rhetoric is different from that of previous administrations on Iran's nuclear capability. Whereas previous administrations made it clear that Iran would not be allowed to deploy nuclear weapons, the Obama administration has subtly changed the message to what it will do "when" Iran deploys nuclear weapons.

As a result of President Obama's ineffectual approach to handling the Iran nuclear issue, a scenario has now been established in which Israel may be forced to unilaterally respond to the threat posed by Iran—a move that could lead to a global economic meltdown by closing down oil production in the Middle East. This scenario would put Russia in the privileged position of being the world's most important oil producer, a thought that should make every American cringe. The hostility of the President and his party to the American oil industry and to the development of our country's natural resources only exacerbates the problem. President Obama is allowing the Russian menace that President Reagan brought down to reassert itself.

Tied closely to his blunders in dealing with Iran is Obama's decision in September 2009 to eliminate the missile shield President Bush put in place to protect Eastern Europe. This move delighted Russian and Iranian officials, a fact that in and of itself should have given the President pause. Without this missile defense system, Eastern Europe is vulnerable to a nuclear attack from Iran and Russia. The President's decision to remove the missile shield over Eastern Europe has been characterized as an example of the weakest possible diplomacy. Obama was criticized for failing the foreign policy *quid pro quo* test by giving up the missile shield without getting anything in return. Small wonder the Russians were so happy about his decision.

Be a Combination of Teddy Roosevelt and Ronald Reagan in Foreign Policy

After four years of President Obama's timidity in foreign policy, Americans will be ready for a president who can restore their confidence and help our nation exert itself in ways that are in its own best interest. Sarah Palin can be that person if she will learn from the foreign-policy records of just two presidents—Teddy Roosevelt and Ronald Reagan.

President Obama has a way with words. In fact, he appears to have inherited President Clinton's propensity for staying in perpetual campaign mode. But words alone are not sufficient when the stability of the world depends in large measure on America's strength and resolve. Teddy Roosevelt knew this when he said, "Speak softly and carry a big stick." His big stick was America's Great White Fleet of battleships. With little support from a timid Congress, he put the fleet on display in a worldwide tour of key ports to send a message to our allies and enemies about American strength and resolve.

Roosevelt was adept at applying both aspects of his foreign policy motto. He knew when it was better to speak softly and when to wield the big stick. For example, he had to use the stick to win approval to build the Panama Canal. When corrupt officials in Bogota, Colombia threatened to derail his plans to build the Canal, Roosevelt sent them a powerful message by deploying the USS Nashville to their shores. They got the message. On another occasion, when Germany and Britain both threatened to occupy Venezuela, Roosevelt called in their ambassadors for a private conversation. Speaking softly, the President explained that any attempt by a European nation to occupy an independent nation in the western hemisphere would be viewed as a violation of the Monroe Doctrine. Thankful he had chosen to use quiet diplomacy, Germany and Britian backed off.

Roosevelt's willingness to wield the big stick coupled with his ability to apply quiet diplomacy when appropriate made him an effective peacemaker. These abilities proved valuable when war broke out between Russia and Japan in 1904. Understanding that world stability was threatened, Roosevelt invited representatives of the two warring nations to New Hampshire for peace talks. Applying quiet diplomacy while holding the big stick behind his back, he was able to gain their acceptance of what came to be known as the Treaty of Portsmouth. Thanks to Teddy Roosevelt, the Russo-Japanese War ended before it could get out of hand and pull the rest of the world into the conflict. As a result of his diplomacy, President Roosevelt became the first American to win the Nobel Peace Prize.

President Reagan was just as forthright and bold in foreign policy. The world took notice when he labeled the Soviet Union an "evil empire." The label, despite protests from liberals, was accurate. Since the days of Stalin, the communists had systematically murdered 40—60 million of their fellow citizens and imprisoned tens of millions more in the infamous gulags. The Soviets certainly understood his meaning when President Reagan said, "Mr. Gorbachev, tear down this wall." Then to back up this courageous statement, he threatened to deploy the Strategic Defense Initiative (SDI). Journalists in America scoffed at the idea calling it "Star Wars." But the Soviet leaders did not scoff. Their already fragile socialist economy teetering on insolvency, SDI frightened the Kremlin's leaders into taking actions that precipitated a national economic meltdown. In spite of the lessons of the Reagan era, President Obama is trying to cut military spending as a way to help fund his socialist energy, economic, and healthcare initiatives.

Contrast the boldness, clarity, and resolve of Presidents Roosevelt and Reagan with the tentative, tepid actions of President Obama. In foreign policy matters, President

Obama calls to mind an image of a latter-day Jimmy Carter, albeit a more articulate version. Even his detractors admit that President Obama is an articulate speaker. He can deliver a moving speech. Unfortunately, the world leaders are not like America's voters—they don't confuse image with substance. Rather, they have the opportunistic, self-interested instincts of a shark for detecting vulnerability and attacking their prey.

If President Obama appears weak or naive, our allies will lose faith in America and make the best deal they can with our enemies. It is already happening. Even the European leaders who claim they like Barack Obama much more than George W. Bush have no illusions about his willingness to stand up to the Russian Bear or the rogue leaders in Iran. The President's decision to remove the nuclear shield over Eastern Europe validated their lack of faith in him. In the meantime, our enemies are doing what sharks always do—circling their prey and looking for opportunities to attack.

In the next election, left-leaning media pundits will once again attempt to portray Sarah Palin as a foreign policy lightweight. They will point out that their favorite son now has four years of foreign policy experience. Sarah Palin should not shrink from the issue. Rather, she should turn it around on the media and the Obama campaign. While it will be true that the President will have four years of experience by the time the next election rolls around, it is equally true that it will have been four years of bad experience characterized by ineptitude, blunders, the weakening of our economic and military might, and apologies.

This is the point Sarah Palin will need to make to the American people using specific examples. Fortunately for her (but unfortunately for Americans), President Obama is hard at work providing those examples. Finally, she might consider beginning every foreign-relations speech with the following promise: "Unlike President Obama, I will never apologize for being an American."

Support the Military

Her support of the military and the fact that, unlike President Obama and most Congressmen, Sarah Palin has a son serving in uniform, will stand her in good stead with the American public in the next presidential election. Our research for this book was able to identify only seven members of Congress who have children serving in the military—six of the seven are Republicans. Of course, the composition of Congress changes over time, as will these numbers. However, the point to understand here is that in a liberal-dominated Congress—the branch of government that declares war—only a few members have children serving their country in the military. In other words, the majority of those who declare war have no personal interest in the fight. This is just one of the many reasons that Congress suffers from a credibility gap with the American public. Sarah Palin has no such problem, a fact that will serve her well.

Although his proposed cuts in military spending were not well-received in Congress, President Obama's support of the military is tepid at best. In fact, one of the biggest challenges he has as President is to make sure that his true intentions and feelings concerning the military are not known by the American public. To date President Obama has wisely avoided any overt conflicts with the military, but make no mistake about it, he is no friend of the armed forces. In fact, a good way to gauge his true position with regard to the Army, Navy, Air Force, Marine Corps, and Coast Guard is to observe how he responds, if at all, when his core supporters—the far left—mistreat men and women in uniform. His response to date has been to turn a blind eye to abuses of the military by the far left.

One of the favorite targets of the radical left is America's armed forces. The radical left hates our military because they want to believe—despite the lessons of history—that man can create peace on earth through dialogue. They fail to understand that our enemies seek dialogue only when we are militarily strong. Attacking the military has long been a staple of the radical left. Following the tragedy of the 9-11 terrorist attacks on the World Trade Center and the Pentagon, our country underwent what appeared to be a transformation. Liberals, conservatives, and moderates pulled together in a show of patriotism. "We Will Never Forget" bumper stickers could be seen displayed on the automobiles of people from both ends of the political spectrum. American flags were proudly displayed and the military was once again afforded a level of respect it had not enjoyed since the end of World War II. Not surprisingly, the national unity that resulted from the terrorist attacks of 9-11 did not last long. Many who claimed they would "never forget," forgot.

Following the 9-11 attacks, members of the radical left

kept a low profile for awhile, perhaps fearing a patriotic backlash or as is more likely the case, simply biding their time. Then, in March of 2003, one of its foot soldiers—Nicholas DeGenova—broke the silence. DeGenova's anti-military activities preceded Barack Obama's presidency, but they are instructive because during the Obama administration such activities have increased. DeGenova, a professor of anthropology and Latino studies at Columbia University, said during a teach-in that he hoped the United States military would suffer a "million Mogadishus."[1]

When his intemperate remarks resulted in a vocal backlash, DeGenova attempted to rescue himself with what President Obama would call "better calibrated" words. In defending his anti-military tirade, DeGenova said:

> In my brief presentation, I outlined a long history of U.S. invasions, wars of conquest, military occupations, and colonization in order to establish that imperialism and white supremacy have been constitutive of U.S. nation-state formation and U.S. nationalism. In that context, I stressed the necessity of repudiating all forms of U.S, patriotism...I emphasized that U.S. troops are indeed confronted with a choice—to perpetuate this war against the Iraqi people or to refuse to fight and contribute toward the defeat of the U.S. war machine. [2]

The professor would have fared better had he just remained silent, but—like most who abhor the military and most radical leftists—remaining silent was not an option for DeGenova. His hatred of the military is so intense that he feels compelled to speak out no matter how inappropriate his remarks.

Attacks on Military Recruiters

Among the left's newest targets are military recruiters. Each branch of the military has a long history of visiting college and university campuses, setting up recruiting booths, and talking with students who might be interested in serving their country. Unfortunately, recruiters on leftwing campuses are easy targets for the obnoxious and even violent tactics of the radical left. What follows are several examples of attacks on military recruiters led by the Campus Antiwar Network (CAN), a group affiliated with an organization called the Socialist Worker. With President Obama in office, CAN and other antimilitary organizations are feeling increasingly empowered.

- "Members of the Campus Antiwar Network (CAN) at the Rochester Institute of Technology (RIT) are celebrating a significant victory after the director for Campus Life issued the order to stop allowing military recruiters in the Student Alumni Union...They may have been banned from the busiest place on campus, but they will find an alternative location to recruit. CAN has no problem with changing accommodations. We'll keep fighting."[3] Obviously, the radical left relishes its attacks on the military. Members of CAN created so much turmoil on the RIT

campus that the institution's administration required recruiters to move to a remote location to
avoid a riot. Notice it was the recruiters and not
the perpetrators of the turmoil who were pun-
ished by the university's liberal administration.
As can be seen from this example, the radical
left is aggressively pursuing an anti-military
agenda and university administrators are aiding
and abetting their actions.

• San Francisco State University held a career fair
on September 25, 2008. Among the partici-
pants were recruiters from the Marine Corps,
Department of Homeland Security, and U.S.
Border Patrol. In a direct attack on the military,
student protesters marched on the recruiting
booths shouting, "What are they recruiting for?
Murder, rape, torture, and war." The protesters
attempted to conduct a sit-in at the recruiting
booths. When their attempts were foiled by
police officers, they staged a rally outside the
building. Eventually some of the protesters were
able to gain admission to the building, at which
point they harassed the Marine recruiters.[4]

• Anti-military students at Seattle Community
College decided to shut down efforts by the military to recruit on campus in November 2008.
Here is how Jorge Torres described the situation
on the website of the Socialist Worker. "When
activists in the Anti-War Collective and the

International Socialist Organization heard two
days ahead of time that Air Force, Army, and
Coast Guard recruiters had all reserved tables
in the school atrium for two hours during the
busiest time of the day, they quickly publicized a
protest by text messaging and passing out fly-
ers. Some 20 students—some who were passing
by—joined the action throughout the two hours.
Students held picket signs, passed out fact sheets
about the military and the lies recruiters tell,
and chanted 'Recruiters off campus!'"[5]

Many Americans are appalled to see the military treated so disgracefully on college and university campuses.
However, having both served in the Marine Corps during
the Vietnam War and experienced first hand some of the
most violent of the anti-war, anti-military protests of that
era, we know this is just the latest chapter in the radical
left's on-going war against the military. It did not stop after
Vietnam. Rather, it simply went into temporary hibernation. The hibernation is over and the left is back to attacking one of its favorite targets—the United States military.

While serving in the Marines, I (David Goetsch) experienced firsthand how deep-seated the anti-military
animosity of leftist college professors can be. It was near
the end of my tour of duty in the Marine Corps and I was
stationed at Camp Pendleton, California. When off duty,
I took night classes at an extension center of a major university. Because of the crunch to make it to class on time, I
often arrived in uniform, although wearing civilian clothes
would not have mattered anyway. With my high-and-tight

Marine Corps haircut, I would never have been confused
for one of my long-haired, tie-dyed classmates. Needless
to say, my Marine Corps demeanor did not endear me to
the anti-war flower children in my class.

I had been warned by other Marines who lived off-base to
expect the worst, and I did experience some of the anti-military bias they had warned me about. I was shunned by my
classmates—none of the other students wanted to be part-
nered with me in the lab, talk with me during breaks, share
class notes, or include me in study groups. There were also
the usual anti-military comments made behind my back, but
in reality, I experienced very little in the way of overt harass-
ment from my classmates. Rather, I appeared to be a curios-
ity to them, something akin to an animal that had escaped
from the zoo and might be dangerous.

The professor was a different story. He took every opportunity to make snide comments about the military in
general and me in particular. In fact, he spent more time
haranguing the military, venting his spleen about the Vietnam War, and encouraging the class to participate in various sit-ins, teach-ins, and protests than he did teaching. The
only way to earn extra-credit in this professor's class was to
join him in some type of anti-military protest. Completely
focused on finishing my college degree, I was willing to put
up with his tirades in order to get through the course and
have the required credits on my transcript. Consequently, I
typically ignored him. However, one night he went too far.

My classmates and I were given fetal pigs to dissect as
a laboratory assignment—one pig for every two students.
My lab partner was a pale, thin young man with long

greasy hair who reeked of marijuana. This poor kid was so nervous about even being near me that when I picked up the scalpel to get started he actually cringed. In addition to his fear of a scalpel-wielding Marine, my lab partner was none too happy about having to cut up the pig. Unsure about how to proceed, he asked the professor for help. The professor responded by saying, "Ask your lab partner. After all, fetal pigs are babies, and Marines know all about cutting up babies."

With great effort, I remained calm but the look on my face must have spoken volumes. When I raised my hand to get his attention, he was clearly uncomfortable acknowledging it, and at first just ignored me. But I persisted. When he saw that I was not going to be put off and finally acknowledged my hand I said, "I would like to speak with you in private please, right now." A hush fell over the class and the professor grew suddenly pale. His hands trembled noticeably. Instead of inviting me into his office for a private conversation, the professor dismissed the class, claiming he felt suddenly ill.

My ride back to Camp Pendleton that night was provided by a friend who was a Navy Corpsman (medic) preparing to go to medical school. During what the Navy calls the "Zumwalt era," he was allowed to wear long hair and a beard. This, of course, allowed him to fit in much better than I could with our classmates. As we made the hour-long drive back to the base, I asked him about the incident in class and why the professor behaved so strangely when I requested a private conference. He laughed sardonically and said, "It's simple. The man is scared to death of you.

These liberals actually believe all of the nonsense they say about you Marines—baby killers and all that. Don't let your guard down though; he will find a way to hurt you. Radicals like this professor hate the military with a passion that defies logic."

After this incident, the anti-military comments from the professor stopped. In fact, he kept his distance and avoided me. But, just as my friend said he would, the professor found an underhanded way to cause me trouble. Knowing from our introductions on the first night of class that I would be finishing my tour of duty in the Marine Corps and going home to Florida right after completing his course, this professor must have felt safe because he gave me an "F" for my final grade. My average for the class was 98.7 percent.

Emboldened by the distance between California and Florida, this leftist professor no doubt decided to strike where he could hurt me most. It took more than six months, many telephone calls to the dean, and several letters from an attorney accompanied by copies of my tests and coursework before I succeeded in having the grade changed. Even then the professor relented only in changing my grade to a "C." I am sure he intuited that since I was not majoring in a scientific discipline and his course was just an elective for me, I would not press the point if I received a passing grade. He was right. All I needed for my degree was a biology course with a "C" or better on my transcript. I was headed for graduate school and had no more time to waste on a radical professor who hated the military so much that he would stoop to such pettiness.

My classmates and I learned very little about biology in this class. Since the professor's lectures invariably devolved into anti-war tirades, the class could have easily passed for a political science course. However, I did learn a valuable lesson about how much the radical left despises the military, how far it will go in pursuit of its anti-military agenda, and how petty it can be in its attacks on what it considers the enemy. And what was true during the Vietnam era is just as true now, perhaps even more so as left-wing secular humanism has become even more dominant on campuses. Sarah Palin will need to hold the left responsible for its anti-military bias during the next presidential campaign while simultaneously demonstrating appropriate concern and respect for military personnel and their families.

Why the Left Attacks America, Conservatives, and the Military

The militancy of the left in conducting its culture war against America, conservatives, and the military is a by-product of its religious philosophy—secular humanism. Secular humanism, as practiced by the radical left, holds that man is naturally good or at least neutral, rather than fallen in sin. If man is naturally good or even neutral he is a product of his environment and can, therefore, be perfected by perfecting his environment. In order to perfect man's environment—as if that could ever be achieved—it is necessary to know which environmental influences are good and which are bad.

Members of the radical left think they know which environmental influences are good and which are bad. Hence, they attempt to bring good environmental influences to bear on individuals and society while eliminating the bad. This sounds reasonable until you consider that it requires: 1) man to decide what is good and bad, and 2) those *in the know*—leftist elites—to have total control over all that influences society. This means they must control government, the public schools, foreign policy, and, of course, the military. The only time leftists don't object to the military is when they want to use it for their own purposes.

If leftists can control America's institutions, they can control America. With this accomplished, perpetuating leftist thinking while silencing the opposition is a much simpler task. Dissenting voices that threaten the left's monopoly are to be silenced no matter what it takes. This is why the left is so militant in carrying out its culture war against America, conservatives, and the military.

Grassroots Americans and the Military

Sarah Palin's views on the military are like those of grassroots Americans—supportive and respectful. Unlike the left, grassroots Americans serve in the military, as do their children and grandchildren. Sarah Palin has a son in the military. This means that like thousands of other American families, her family has a personal interest in the fight. For Sarah Palin and other parents of military personnel, national defense is not an abstract concept. It is a hard reality that frequently brings them to their knees in prayer and causes them to swell with pride every time they see the American flag waving freely. The maxim that nobody appreciates freedom more than those who fight for it also applies to the parents of those who fight for freedom.

Support of and respect for the military must be made an issue in the next election, and President Obama must not be allowed to get away with condoning the type of anti-military attitudes and actions that have become prevalent during his administration. Leftists who attack the military are among the principal benefactors of the freedom and liberty for which so many Americans have fought and died, and for which our troops serve today. To allow leftist dissenters to get away with hypocritically attacking military personnel who put their lives on the line defending the right of dissent is unacceptable. The left does not have to agree with the military or even serve but it should respect and honor those who put their lives on the line in defense of freedom and liberty. Because she has a personal stake in the issue, Sarah Palin has the credibility to make sure this message is heard.

Attitudes of Grassroots Americans Toward Servicemen and Women

A friend recently shared a story that illustrates how grassroots Americans—those for whom Sarah Palin has the strongest appeal—feel about the men and women who serve our country in uniform. The story is titled "Sack Lunches." We cannot verify its veracity, but can imagine that it is just one of a hundred such stories that occur every day somewhere in America.

> I lifted my carry-on bag into the luggage compartment and sat down in my assigned seat. It was going to be a long flight. Just

before take-off, a group of soldiers came
down the aisle and filled all the remaining
seats. They were probably flying on stand-
by status. I decided to start a conversation.
"Where are you headed?" I asked a soldier
seated nearby. "Petawawa. We'll be there
for two weeks of special training, and then
we deploy to Afghanistan."

After about an hour, a steward announced that sack lunches were available
for five dollars. It would be several hours
before we reached our destination so I decided to purchase a sack lunch. As I reached
for my wallet, I overhead a soldier ask his
buddy if he planned to buy lunch. "No, five
bucks is too much money for just a sack
lunch. I'll wait until we get to the base." His
friend agreed.

I looked around at the other soldiers
and saw that none were buying lunch. Concerned, I walked to the back of the plane,
handed the flight attendant a fifty dollar bill,
and asked her to take a lunch to the soldiers.
She grabbed my arm and squeezed tightly.
Her eyes brimming with tears, she thanked
me and said, "My son was a soldier in Iraq."
Picking up ten lunch sacks, she headed up
the aisle to where the soldiers were seated.

After eating, I went to the back of the
plane, heading for the restroom. A man

stopped me. "I saw what you did and want to be part of it. Here, take this." He handed me twenty-five dollars. Soon after I returned to my seat, I saw the Flight Captain coming down the aisle, looking at the numbers as he walked. When he got to my row he stopped, smiled, and said, "I want to shake your hand."

Quickly unfastening my seatbelt I stood and took the Captain's hand. With a booming voice he said, "I was a soldier once and a military pilot. Somebody bought me a lunch one time. It was an act of kindness I never forgot." I felt a little embarrassed when the passengers applauded. Later I walked to the front of the plane to stretch my legs. A man who was seated about six rows in front of me reached out to shake my hand. He left twenty-five dollars in my palm.

When we landed I gathered my belongings and started to deplane. Another passenger stopped me and wordlessly put something in my shirt pocket. It was another twenty-five dollars. In the terminal, the soldiers were gathering for their trip to the base. I walked over and handed them the seventy-five dollars that had been donated. "It might be a while before you reach the base. Have something to eat, and God bless you."

Ten young men left that flight feeling the love and respect of their fellow travelers. Walking to my car, I whispered a prayer for their safe return. These soldiers were giving their all for our country. All my fellow passengers and I could only give them was a couple of meals. It seemed so little. A veteran is someone who, at one point in his life, wrote a blank check made payable to "The United States of America" for an amount "up to and including my life." Too many people take this incredibly unselfish act of devotion to duty, honor, and country for granted.

Whether this story is factual or not, the sentiments it expresses certainly are. Grassroots Americans do respect our military personnel and they do not like to see them treated poorly by arrogant members of the left who loudly demand their Constitutional rights and then attack those who fight and die defending those rights. When a young person writes a blank check for an amount "up to and including my life," he or she deserves respect. Sarah Palin knows this, believes it, and lives it. Her respect and support for the military and the fact that she has a personal interest in the fight, when the President and most members of Congress do not, will serve her well in the next election, as will her core values, commitment to America's best interests, and moral courage.

NOTES

1. "Nicholas DeGenova Explains What he Meant When he Called for a Million Mogadishus." Retrieved from http://hnn.us/articles/1396.html on January 29, 2009.

2. *Ibid.*

3. "Recruiters banned at RIT." Retrieved from http://socialistworker.org/2009/01/19/recruiters-banned-at-RIT on January 30, 2009.

4. Kristin Lubbert, "Protesting the recruiters at SFSU." Retrieved from http://socialist worker.org/2009/09/29/protesting-recruiters-at-SFSU on January 30, 2009.

5. Jorge Torres, "Seattle protest against recruiters," *Activist News.* Retrieved from http://socialworker.org/2008/12/02seattle-protest-against-recruiters on January 30, 2009.

Six

Hold Obama Accountable

*"The United States—the world's great bastion
of freedom—is sliding toward socialism.
High-profile bailouts and a stimulus bill have toppled
the walls between government and the private sector."*

—Senator Jim DeMint
Saving Freedom

Barack Obama became president by appealing to his solid core of supporters on the left and a sufficient number of independents and moderates in the middle. He did this by promising change without being specific concerning what he meant by the term. Now that he is in office, many of the moderates and independents who supported him are beginning to wonder if they made a mistake. The more they learn about the changes President Obama wants to make, the less his middle-of-the-road supporters like them. Many have become so alarmed at his affinity for socialist economic policies that they now question if President Obama truly has the best interests of America at heart. Some are even beginning to wonder if he is really an American at all.

Many Americans, including independents and moderates who supported him, are now concerned that President Obama is determined to transform the United States into a European-style socialist state, or worse. The president's own policies and programs do little to dispel this concern. To Obama's independent and moderate supporters, his promise of "change" sounded good until they began to learn what he actually meant. Now they not only question his policies and programs, they question his allegiance to capitalism, the free market, and traditional American values.

More than any other strategy presented in this book, holding President Obama accountable for his socialist policies and broken promises is a must for Sarah Palin in the next presidential election. It is no overstatement to say that President Obama's love affair with socialism frightens Americans or that his broken promises frustrate them. Many moderates and independents who supported Barack Obama now feel betrayed by him. This fact gives Sarah Palin an opportunity to win the White House using a formula that is a mirror image of the one that put Barack Obama in the Oval Office: 1) hold her conservative base of support, and 2) win over the moderates and independents who now wonder if they erred in supporting Barack Obama.

Smiling Socialists and the Damage They Can Do to America

In his book, *Welcome to Obamaland: I have Seen your Future and it Doesn't Work*, British journalist James Delingpole sends an ominous message to all Americans. "This would be my first warning to you: if you think your new president and his ... Democratic majorities in both houses of Congress can't do any serious harm to your vast, resilient country, that their socialist bromides might not, in the end, mark 'the end of the American idea' (to quote Mark Steyn)—well, you're quite wrong. Smiling socialists can do a great deal of damage indeed."[1]

Delingpole's book summarizes the state of Great Britain's economy and British society in general in the wake of Tony Blair's socialist retreat from the hard-won reforms of Margaret Thatcher's administration. "Our economy is in ruins. We're afraid, and understandably so, for of all the G7 nations, our economy has officially been named the feeblest, the most out-of-control, and the one least likely to make a quick recovery from the global depression."[2] His observations about British society during the Blair administration paint an even bleaker picture:

- Knife and gun crime increased

- Food and fuel costs skyrocketed

- The railroad system collapsed

- Hospitals became filthy and overcrowded

- School standards plummeted

- British universities became a joke [3]

Delingpole describes how the everyday freedoms of British citizens in "the world's oldest democracy were increasingly circumscribed by petty, micromanaging, nanny-ish laws governing every aspect of our behavior from the games our kids could play at school, to the kind of light bulbs we could use, to how often we could dispose of our trash, to the sort of jokes it was permissible to tell. We'd gone, in a terrifyingly short space, from being a thriving capitalist state to a failed socialist experiment."[4]

Where President Obama is Trying to Take Our Country

Because President Obama and his leftist supporters can nonchalantly introduce socialist laws, programs, and policies without raising so much as a word of caution from the fawning press corps, we believe it is important to ask: Where is President Obama trying to take our country? Americans need to be clear that the President is determined to transform what has long been the world's most powerful capitalist economy into a socialist system based on the concept of redistribution of wealth. Further, Americans need to understand exactly what this inoffensive-sounding concept actually means to our country and to them personally.

If defined strictly from an economic perspective, socialism is a centrally-planned economy in which the government controls all of the means of production, distribution, and commerce and seeks to make all people economically and socially equal. However, defining socialism as simply an economic system falls well short of full disclosure. Socialism is more than just an economic system. It is an economic system that is part of a broader worldview—a worldview in which the state is god and the power of government is used to take from productive people and give to those who are less productive, under the guise of "redistribution of wealth." What sounds like charity is actually government coercion.

Robert Heilbroner, a socialist for most his life before seeing the light, describes socialism as "the tragic failure of the twentieth century."[5]   Originally envisioned as a remedy for what was viewed by some as the defects of capitalism, socialism has failed dismally everywhere it has been tried. Writing about socialism, Helibroner says: "[I]t has far surpassed capitalism in both economic malfunction and moral cruelty. Yet the idea and the ideal of socialism linger on. Whether socialism in some form will eventually return as a major organizing force in human affairs is unknown, but no one can accurately appraise its prospects who has not taken into account the dramatic story of its rise and fall."[6]

A Brief History of Socialism

Socialism's birth is typically attributed to Karl Marx but, in fact, he wrote only a few pages about the concept in his well-known work, The Communist *Manifesto*. In the modern era, the most prominent advocates of socialism include Robert Owen, Charles Fourier, Pierre-Joseph Proudon, Louis Blanc, Charles Hall, and Saint-Simon. This group criticized what they saw as the inequities of the Industrial Revolution. To remedy these perceived inequities they advocated a more egalitarian redistribution of wealth and a reordering of society into small utopian communities in which there would be no private property. Private property and the right of the owners to control the use of their property, of course, are fundamental tenets of capitalism.

Socialistic thinking has been prevalent in Europe—as well as in some quarters in America—since the late 19th century. Socialists throughout Europe dominated the universities, influenced the thinking of intellectuals, and encouraged the spread of socialism in every way possible. The Fabian Socialists of England were especially effective in bringing democratic socialism to that country.

They also influenced socialist thinking in America. The Fabians sought to bring about the acceptance and spread of socialism by gradual means, beginning with scholarly works on economic history, and using popular literature to influence public opinion. Working in tandem with other socialist groups, the Fabians played a key role in the establishment of the British welfare state. This same *boil-the-frog* approach had been used by socialists in the United States until Barack Obama was elected. At this point, things changed overnight. As a President with a majority in Congress, Barack Obama chose to ram as much socialist legislation through Congress as he could while still in a position to do so, all the while denying that his bills were socialist in nature.

In the United States, socialism was prominent in the thinking of rationalistic New England and Northern reformers. For example, the first "free" public schools were established by Unitarian socialists who wanted to use them as vehicles for undermining Christianity, changing America's cultural values, and promoting the acceptance of socialism. This is an important point for Americans to understand and one that Sarah Palin should make repeatedly during her campaign for the presidency. Socialism has never been only about economics. It is a much broader worldview concept, and one that has been aided by European immigration. Nineteenth and twentieth century immigration, particularly from Germany, brought a wave of socialists to America. In the process, classical, small-government liberalism was transformed into big-government democratic socialism.

Nationalistic socialists of the 1880s and 1890s, like the Fabians, sought to achieve the spread of socialism gradually and peacefully through increased government control. Arguing that political equality is meaningless without economic equality, they had a powerful influence on many middle-class Americans. This is the very argument that President Obama uses to promote his socialist programs. At the same time, Christian Socialism and the Social Gospel movement influenced many Christians in the old mainline Protestant denominations from the 1880s through the 1920s. Those who were influenced by the Social Gospel attacked business, supported organized labor, promoted the notion that social justice requires economic equality, and endorsed socialist policies and candidates.

In politics, the 1890s and 1900s saw the emergence and growth in America of the Socialist Party and the Socialist Labor Party. The "Progressives" of the early 20th century were strongly influenced by socialism. Consequently, they expected government to exercise more control over business, and adopted—to some extent—socialist programs. Intellectuals in politics used their influence to encourage the acceptance and spread of socialism during these years. For example, President Woodrow Wilson—the former professor and college president—advanced socialist thinking through his teaching, public oratory, and policies during World War I. His "Fourteen Points" and League of Nations were precursors to President Obama's support of international treaties that supersede the Constitution and his one-world concept in international relations.

Later, Franklin Roosevelt, with help from his left-wing

"Brain Trust", a Democrat-controlled Congress, and *me-too* Republicans, laid the foundation for American socialism with his New Deal policies, programs, and Supreme Court appointments. Subsequent presidents, Congresses, and liberal Supreme-Court majorities—aided and abetted by left-wing intellectuals in colleges, universities, and the entertainment industry—slowly but steadily advanced the spread of socialism in America. There was opposition, of course. But as it always does when opposition arises, the left deftly applied the concept of boiling the frog so that progress was slow enough to go unnoticed by the majority of Americans. Leftists also masked the socialist nature of their programs by giving them attractive, but deceptive titles.

Socialism really got a boost when it was adopted by Lenin following the Russian Revolution in which Czar Nicholas was overthrown and his family murdered. Having defeated the Russian aristocracy, Lenin's now-powerful followers had a free hand and no need to compromise with political opponents. Socialists everywhere applauded Lenin's—and socialism's—ascension to power and eagerly awaited the results of what they referred to as the "great experiment."

Having seized power in Russia, Lenin found himself in the uncomfortable position of having to follow through on his promises to make things better. Lenin believed that a nation's economy would perform better with centralized state control of production, distribution, and commerce and without what he thought of as the negative influences of the profit motive and competition. Predictably, Lenin's attempt to apply socialist principles on a broad scale failed miserably. Just four years after the establishment of a socialist economy, production in the Soviet Union had fallen to only a fraction of its rate prior to the revolution. In fact, Lenin's experiment with socialism was such an abysmal failure that he was forced to choose between the Soviet people starving and reinstituting the free-market incentives of capitalism, albeit on a limited basis. He opted for limited capitalism under what was called the *New Economic Program* (NEP).

This is where things stood when Lenin died and Stalin assumed the reins of power. Stalin and his successors, until the collapse of the Soviet Union, based the country's economy on state planning of production based on a pyramid model. At the peak of the pyramid, the state planning agency established broad targets and directives. These targets and directives cascaded down through a succession of ministries and regional planning organizations that, in turn, passed them down to factories. In the factories, the plans were reviewed by the factory managers and engineers who were expected to implement them. [7]

Lenin's misguided experiment with socialism stumbled along for approximately 70 years—a textbook example of mass inefficiency and waste—until the Soviet Union's socialist economy gasped its last breath and finally collapsed. Without massive and repeated infusions of economic aid from the United States and the countries of Western Europe in the form of technology and expertise—including factories and the technicians to run them—the failure of the "great experiment" would have occurred even sooner.

Heilbroner describes the collapse of the Soviet Union's

doomed socialist economy in stark terms:

> It is not surprising that this increasingly
> Byzantine system began to create serious
> dysfunctions beneath the overall statistics
> of growth. During the 1960s the Soviet
> Union became the first industrial country in
> history to suffer a prolonged peacetime fall
> in average life expectancy, a symptom of its
> disastrous misallocation of resources. Mili-
> tary research facilities could get whatever
> they needed, but hospitals were low on the
> priority list. By the 1970s the figures clearly
> indicated a slowing of overall production.
> By the 1980s the Soviet Union officially ac-
> knowledged a near end to growth that was,
> in reality, an unofficial decline. In 1987 the
> first official law embodying *perestroika*—
> restructuring—was put into effect. Presi-
> dent Mikhail Gorbachev announced his in-
> tention to revamp the economy from top to
> bottom by introducing the market, reestab-
> lishing private ownership, and opening the
> system to free economic interchange with
> the West. Seventy years of socialist rise had
> come to an end.[8]

Socialism has been tried many times by many different nations over many years. Throughout all of this, it has
been consistent in its record of failure. Christian philosopher D. Elton Trueblood demonstrated that a centrally-

planned economy requires the planners to know: 1) what resources are immediately available, 2) what resources will be available in the future, 3) what consumers want now, and 4) what consumers will want in the future.[9] Of course, this means that central planners must be aware of market factors that are impossible to know; factors that only God can know. In a free-market economy, factors such as prices, profits, and losses provide the information needed to respond quickly to market opportunities and threats and to change plans in response to the ever-changing conditions of the market. This is one of the reasons why a free-market economy works more efficiently than a socialist economy.

Socialism is More Than Just a Misguided Economic System

Socialism is a failed concept even when viewed strictly from the perspective of economics. However, when viewed in the broader context of a worldview, the truth about this unworkable concept becomes even more disturbing. In order to accept the socialist worldview, you must accept the premise that the state knows better than the individual how people should live and what people should believe. The highest authority to a socialist is the all-knowing, all-powerful, all-authoritative state. In other words, to a socialist the state is god. As god, the state controls all aspects of life. Just as Christians worship the God of the Bible, socialists worship the state.

This state-as-god mentality is why socialists willingly submit to centralized government control of not just the economy, but all aspects of their lives—what they should believe, how they should live, and what they should think. Hence, socialism is a religious philosophy based on faith in man's providence; a worldview that replaces God's divine providence with faith in man's ability to ensure his own salvation. Faith is the substance of things hoped for and the proof of things unseen, and faith is why socialists stubbornly cling to their misguided views in spite of the concept's long record of failure.

Inherent Shortcomings of Socialism

Consider just a few of socialism's inherent shortcomings. Socialism does not, will not, and cannot work because it:

- Appeals to the base aspects of human nature

- Replaces the family as the central unit in society with the state

- Allows legalized theft in the name of redistribution of wealth to achieve "social justice."

- Encourages sloth instead of diligence

- Rewards irresponsibility, laziness, and a lack of accountability

- Encourages self-indulgence instead of self-reliance

- Encourages the shifting of personal responsibility to others

- Replaces the self-discipline of deferred gratification with the desire for instant gratification

- Undermines the values associated with the entrepreneurial spirit and the traditional work ethic (*i.e.* thrift, diligence, self-reliance, self-discipline, responsibility, accountability, deferred gratification, and hard work) and replaces them with an entitlement mentality

- Treats those who contribute to the betterment of society the same as those who do not even when they are capable of doing so. One might even say it treats contributors worse than those who do not contribute, because it takes from them what they have earned

- Promotes a *get-something-for-nothing* mentality that undermines the moral character of the individual and society

- Robs people of initiative, drive, and ambition as well as wealth

- Undermines the spirit of entrepreneurship and competitiveness

- Promotes totalitarianism, thereby undermining freedom and liberty

In a radio broadcast prior to the British general election of 1945, Winston Churchill said this about socialism: "A socialist policy is abhorrent to the British ideas of freedom. Socialism is inseparably interwoven with totalitarianism and… worship of the state. It will prescribe for everyone where they are to work, what they are to work at, where they may go, and what they may say. Socialism is an attack on the right to breathe freely." [10]

Scriptural Flaws of Socialism

As flawed as socialism is when viewed strictly from an economic perspective, it fares even worse as a worldview. What follows are some of the scriptural flaws of socialism. Socialism:

- Violates the First Commandment by replacing God with the state. As part of its state-as-god perspective, socialism replaces God's never-changing laws with man's ever-changing social mores, or with the desires of socialist manipulators concerning man's mores.

- Violates the Second Commandment in that it worships man and idolizes his fickle desires.

- Violates the Third Commandment by advocating man's right to blaspheme God or to profess Christ while simultaneously promoting laws and practices that violate God's law.

- Violates the Fourth Commandment by denigrating God's admonition to work six days while keeping the Sabbath holy and reserving the day for worship, rest, and fellowship. It also denigrates work by treating idlers in the same way as productive people who contribute more to society.

- Violates the Fifth Commandment by undermining families, undercutting parental authority, attacking traditional marriage, and supporting laws that take for the state that which should be passed from generation to generation by inheritance.

• Violates the Sixth Commandment by legalizing murder in the forms of abortion, infanticide, and euthanasia, all of which have been or are legally practiced in socialist countries, and all of which are supported by the left in America.

• Violates the Seventh Commandment by replacing the definition of justice from God's Law with "social justice" or equality of income and wealth; and by legalizing theft through taxation under the banner of redistributing wealth.

• Violates the Eighth Commandment by de facto condoning adultery with policies and practices that promote sexual promiscuity and indiscriminate sexual indulgence.

• Violates the Ninth Commandment by promoting class warfare that leads to the bearing of false witness against neighbors (*e.g.* portraying the wealthy as exploiters of the poor, using political rhetoric that promotes class envy and strife).

• Violates the Tenth Commandment by promoting covetousness through class envy, advocating the redistribution of wealth, and encouraging an entitlement mentality.

Denying the Evidence of
Socialism's Inherent Flaws

As they push the government ever closer to nationalizing banks, automobile manufacturers, insurance companies, healthcare, education, and energy production, left-leaning politicians are ignoring incontrovertible evidence of the inherent flaws of socialism. Socialism cannot work in a world where the ability to compete in the global arena is so large a factor in determining a nation's quality of life. It does not and cannot work because of three inherent and irreversible flaws: 1) it presupposes that man rather than God governs history, 2) it presupposes that God will not judge socialist societies and governments for violating his holy laws, and 3) it appeals to the worst aspects of human nature. For evidence of this fact, one need only look at the situation that now exists in Europe as a result of socialist government policies and the socialist mindset of the people.

Britain is not alone in allowing socialism to hold it back in the battle of the marketplace waged every day by the competitive nations of the world. Because of their socialist economies, European countries are like sprinters who must drag an anchor behind them as they race against fleet, unencumbered runners from India, China, Japan, and Korea. Britain and the other European nations have descended into socialism and, despite the disastrous results brought by this failed concept, America is blindly following their lead. Socialism has failed everywhere it has been tried and yet left-leaning politicians continue to promote it. What these politicians refuse to acknowledge is that socialism fails because it is inherently flawed, not because Europeans have failed to effectively apply its principles.

> According to a recent study by the Organi-
> zation for Economic Cooperation and De-
> velopment, the average working American
> spends 1,976 hours a year on the job. The
> average German works just 1,535—22 per-
> cent less. The Dutch and Norwegians put
> in even fewer hours. Even the British do 10
> percent less work than their trans-Atlantic
> cousins. As stark as they are, these figures
> understate the extent of European idleness,
> because a larger proportion of Americans
> work. Unemployment rates in most North-
> ern European countries are also markedly
> higher than those in the United States.
> Then there are the strikes. Between 1992
> and 2001, the Spanish economy lost, on
> average, 271 days per 1,000 employees as a
> result of strikes. For Denmark, Italy, Fin-
> land, Ireland and France, the figures range
> between 80 and 120 days.[11]

Consider the impact of these facts in the global arena.
While Europeans are idle, workers in Japan, China, India,
and Korea are producing. To make matters worse, even
when they are working Europeans are less productive than
their Asian competitors because of their poor work ethic—
a product of the socialist mindset.

Capitalism works—albeit imperfectly—because it appeals to and rewards many of the positive elements of hu-

man nature and rests on a foundation of positive values (*i.e.* thrift, diligence, self-reliance, self-discipline, responsibility, accountability, deferred gratification, and hard work as well as initiative, ambition, perseverance, entrepreneurship, etc.).   Socialism does not work because it appeals to and rewards the negative elements of human nature (*i.e.* sloth, laziness, dependence on others, irresponsibility, lack of ambition, covetousness, etc.). Capitalism rewards those who pull the economic wagon. Socialism rewards those who ride in it. Those on the left who deny this inherent flaw of socialism are blinded by political bias and partisan prejudice. They think that socialism will work simply because they want it to.

Using False Compassion to Promote Socialism

One of the most effective, albeit hypocritical, tools used by the left to sell socialism to the American public is compassion—false compassion. This is President Obama's principal strategy in trying to win support for his healthcare plan. Aided and abetted by the media, the left claims to be more compassionate toward the "victims" of society—a message that plays well to Americans encouraged by teachers, trial lawyers, and government bureaucrats to view themselves as victims. However, the truth is that conservatives give a much higher percentage of their personal income to charity than do liberals. For a complete accounting of this little-known fact, see *Who Really Cares: The Surprising Truth about Compassionate Conservatism* (New York: Basic Books, 2006) by Arthur C. Brooks.

In fact, with the assistance of the media and civil trial lawyers liberals have turned victimhood into one of
America's most prosperous industries. Unfortunately, the
so-called compassion of the left is the type that gives in to
the alcoholic who begs for a drink or the addict who pleads
for a fix. Giving in will stop the withdrawal symptoms for
the moment but make the addiction worse in the long run.
The unavoidable result of this advocacy of victimhood is
the encouragement of dependence and entitlement.

The left has mastered the art of *compassion rhetoric*
and uses it effectively to sell socialism to gullible Americans in much the same way a snake-oil salesman hawks his
fraudulent wares. One of the left's favorite terms for selling socialism is *equality.* "Equality" has become the mantra of the left. After all, didn't Thomas Jefferson advocate
equality for all men in the Declaration of Independence?
Didn't Jefferson say that "all men are created equal"? Historians still debate whether Jefferson meant that all men
are created equal before God or before the law. But there
are no serious scholars who believe he meant what the left
means by equality: *equality of outcome rather than opportunity.* The left advocates, legislates, and intimidates in its
on-going attempts to guarantee equality of outcomes in
society regardless of merit or effort. Anyone on the right
who dares claim that an unproductive member of society
deserves less than a productive member is quickly labeled
"hard-hearted" or "mean-spirited."

The left also likes to use the term *fairness* when selling socialism. However, the left's deliberately vague definition of *fairness* clearly violates God's definition of the term.

God's law—the only perfect and unchanging standard—prohibits civil government—as well as anyone else, rich or poor—from engaging in legalized theft. Since civil government is supposed to be a ministry of God, a function of which is to protect those who do good from those who do evil (Romans 13), civil government, more than any other entity, is prohibited from engaging in theft.

Although most of the politicians who promote big-government and socialism are themselves quite wealthy, they like to play the class card when arguing for socialism. They pit the so-called have-nots of society against the haves, conveniently ignoring their own status as haves. Their favorite tactic is to portray the haves as ogres and the have-nots as victims, regardless of how long and hard the haves had to work for the material success they now enjoy or how much their work has benefitted others. The radical left—Obama's most reliable base of support—claims it is "unfair" for a thrifty, diligent, self-reliant producer who pulls America's economic wagon to have more than a lazy, irresponsible, entitled person who only rides in the wagon.

Using Emotionalism to Sell Americans on Socialism

Next to false compassion, emotionalism is the most effective tool of President Obama and his supporters for selling socialism to gullible Americans, and healthcare is the issue around which they build their most emotional arguments. Socialists believe that healthcare should be free and universally available to everyone, regardless of their ability to pay. "Free" universal healthcare is the five-hundred pound

gorilla on the list of President Obama's most important issues. Regardless of how things turn out with this issue
once the dust in Congress settles, Barack Obama will never stop pursuing so-called free universal healthcare until
he is out of office. And you have to give it to the left, on
the surface this is an appealing concept. Few things are
closer to the hearts of Americans than their health and the
health of their loved ones.

This is why emotionalism is such an effective tool for
socialists pushing the universal healthcare agenda. But
there is a problem here that socialists like to ignore. Nothing is free, and especially not healthcare. In fact, few things
are more expensive than healthcare. Even with all of its
abundance, America has finite resources. There are simply not sufficient resources in this or any other country to
provide high-quality universal healthcare that is paid for
by taxpayers. When economists point out this undeniable
fact, socialists immediately fall back on emotionalism and
portray the naysayers as "hard-hearted" capitalists who
don't care about their fellow human beings. This is an excellent example of a key difference between a socialist and
a capitalist. Socialists envision a utopian world and think
it can be achieved simply because they want it to. Capitalists are better students of human nature. Consequently,
they temper their dreams with reality and do much more
to achieve increased prosperity for all—a couple of points
Sarah Palin should incorporate in her campaign rhetoric.

One of the realities capitalists should always keep in
mind is the limited nature of resources. Any time there
are limited resources, decisions must be made and some-

times they can be hard decisions. In every other aspect of our lives, people understand that those who can afford more in the way of material advantages will have them. This is the nature of life. But socialists like to play the class card and label this fact of life unfair. Putting aside the fact that life itself *is* unfair because of man's sinful nature, what is wrong with an individual who contributes more to the economy being able to secure better healthcare in the same way he is able to secure a bigger house and nicer car? After all, even socialists understand this concept.

For example, ask yourself where the wealthy politicians in Washington, D.C. live, what kind of cars they drive, and where they send their children to school. So what is different about healthcare? The answer to this question is simple: *emotional appeal.* Healthcare appeals to people on such a personal level that wealthy leftists can use it to build an ever-growing constituent base of poor people by questioning the fairness of a system that treats the rich and the poor differently. The hard truth—and socialists do not like hard truths—is that when you have universal demand but finite resources the fairest system is the free-market system.

What the emotionalism of socialists conveniently glosses over is that in its own imperfect way, the free-market system results in better healthcare for the poor, the wealthy, and those in the middle—just as it results in better cars, homes, food, and everything else needed by human beings. This is because the free market provides incentives to be productive, while socialism provides no such incentives. On the most fundamental level, the free-market system gives people the incentive to improve themselves economically so they and their families can enjoy better healthcare, homes, cars, food, and all of the other human material necessities. Socialism, on the other hand, provides no such incentives. Why work hard to improve your economic circumstances when you have a "right" to the same socio-economic advantages as someone who contributes more to society and the economy? Worse yet, why should those who now work hard and contribute more to the economy continue to do so when, under socialism, they will no longer benefit from their effort?

Socialists are uncomfortable with the logic contained in these questions. Consequently, upon hearing these kinds of questions they typically respond with their favorite knee-jerk comeback—one that is virtually dripping with emotional appeal: "You think you are better than everyone else." The relative worth of individual human beings is not even the issue here. Christians know that all people stand equally unclothed before God as sinners, which is precisely why it is best to let the free market, rather than the state, make difficult economic choices for us. When the free market chooses, the issue is not who is better, but who has worked long, hard, and smart enough to have the resources to be able to afford more.

Of course there are people whose wealth is inherited, people who have done nothing to deserve the advantages they enjoy in a free-market system. In fact, many of them are left-leaning politicians who hypocritically push a socialist agenda—Senators Ted Kennedy (deceased) and John Kerry come to mind. Advocates of socialist programs like to use emotionalism to claim it is unfair that a poor person receives less of some human necessity than a wealthy person. According to socialists, this is just not fair. However, these same socialists are unable to explain why they think it is fair that someone who contributes less to the economy should be entitled to the same benefits as someone who contributes more.

Left-leaning politicians such as President Obama and his supporters claim to be more compassionate than free-market proponents, but their emotional appeals for "fairness" are just empty words. If they really wanted to be fair, they would be more charitable with their own substantial wealth, rather than taxing middle-income Americans who work hard to provide for themselves and their families. It is easy to be "compassionate" with someone else's money. But where is the fairness when left-leaning politicians live in the most exclusive neighborhoods and send their children to the best private schools while taxing hard-working middle-class Americans who can neither live in exclusive neighborhoods nor send their children to expensive private schools? This is the hypocrisy of the left, President Obama's most ardent supporters.

Government Control as an Instrument of Socialist Control

Christians have faith in God, but socialists have faith only in the state. In fact, to a socialist the state is god. This misguided faith in government is difficult to comprehend until one understands the ultimate goal of socialists—complete control. Socialists seek to control every aspect of the individual's life, and to a socialist the state is the

ultimate instrument of control. Mark Levin, author of Liberty and Tyranny: A Conservative *Manifesto*, explains how
socialists seek to control America by building a "culture of
conformity and dependency, where the ideal citizen takes
on drone-like qualities in service to the state, the individual must be drained of uniqueness and self-worth, and de-
terred from independent thought or behavior."[12]

History and experience show that big government is
inherently inefficient. The reason for this inefficiency goes
beyond just size—although students of organizational behavior know that big is typically synonymous with inefficient. Even in the private sector, organizations tend to lose
efficiency as they grow. However, the private sector at least
has the marketplace to enforce discipline. The government, on the other hand, is ruled by politics not markets,
and politics is the least-disciplined concept known to man.

As President Obama and his supporters continue to
push America down the slippery slope of socialism, as the
federal government continues to grow, and as the federal
debt continues to spiral out of control, the types of pro-
ductivity-sapping inefficiencies associated with the former
Soviet Union are beginning to be seen in the United States.
This is how Mark Levin describes America's rapidly-grow-
ing, increasingly-centralized government: "It administers
a budget of over $3 trillion. It churns out a mind-numbing
number of rules that regulate energy, the environment,
business, labor, employment, transportation, housing, ag-
riculture, food, drugs, education, etc. Even the slightest
human activity apparently requires its intervention: cloth-
ing labels on women's dresses, cosmetic ingredients, and

labeling. It even reaches into the bathroom, mandating showerhead flow rates and allowable gallons per flush for toilets. It sets flammability standards for beds."[13]

This intrusive, oppressive approach to governing is what excites socialists. They see it as their most effective means of control, and it certainly is that. The type of oppressive government that socialists advocate undermines initiative, ambition, free-thought, the work ethic, freedom, liberty, and the entrepreneurial spirit. This is why so many people question if President Obama is really an American at heart. Even the most liberal presidents in the past have not advocated government so burdensome that it undermines the very freedom, attitude, and spirit which made America great.

Among the many problems associated with big government, one stands out above the rest: it does not work. James Delingpole uses Great Britain's National Health System to make this point: "Quite simply, government can never run any service as efficiently as private enterprise can. For one thing, it operates on a scale too unwieldy. The British National Health Service is the world's largest employer after the Chinese army and the Indian State Railway... In 2007-2008 the British National Health Service swallowed up 95 billion pounds—more than any other government department. For this, the taxpayer gets a 'service' so lamentably poor that 55 percent of senior doctors pay for private medical insurance rather than run the risk of having to expose themselves to the NHS's tender care."[14]

Blind Faith of President Obama
and His Supporters in Socialism

The evidence of socialism's failure is conclusive and undeniable to any objective observer. Why then do socialists cling so stubbornly to their *state-as-god* mentality? Of course, socialists are anything but objective observers, but the reasons behind their stubborn adherence to socialist orthodoxy go well beyond a lack of objectivity. David Limbaugh calls this socialist mentality "beltway arrogance and blind faith."[15] Socialists criticize Christians for having what they describe as "blind faith in God," yet President Obama and his supporters cling to their socialist notions—in spite of their perfect record of failure—out of blind faith. In making his point about beltway arrogance and blind faith, Limbaugh cites the example of Congressman Charles Rangel, one of the left's most vocal champions of socialist programs: "Rep. Charles Rangel's recent comments about President Obama's budget exemplify the liberal ruling class's Beltway arrogance and blind faith in an ideology that compels it to press on the accelerator as we head for the cliff toward the nation's financial ruin."[16]

In an interview with Chris Wallace on *Fox News Sunday,* Representative Rangel claimed that he was not troubled by a report from the Congressional Budget Office estimating that President Obama's federal budget deficit would be $2.3 trillion higher than the already astronomically-high projections of the White House.[17] According to Limbaugh, what Rangel meant by his lack of concern was that: "We liberals are going to do what we have been itching to do for decades, and even though our policies will

place even greater burdens on the economy, retard economic growth, and cause the debt and deficits to further
explode, we'll end up with a surplus anyway because we
are so doggone virtuous with our liberal compassion that
fate will have to reward us."[18] Leftists are what Thomas
Sowell calls "the anointed." They believe that they have
been anointed to rule over everyone else.

Arrogance, false compassion, emotionalism, and blind
faith in a system that not only does not work but breeds
laziness, sloth, and irresponsibility—are the characteristics necessary to accept President Obama's socialist programs. Until America replaces these characteristics with
those that support entrepreneurship and the traditional
work ethic—thrift, diligence, self-reliance, self-discipline,
responsibility, accountability, deferred gratification, and
hard work—all the government programs in the world will
have no more effect than water that is poured into a leaky
bucket. In the age of global competition, America cannot win with an inefficient, government-controlled, leaky
bucket economy.

Socialists claim to want to help people, but their claim
cannot stand up to the scrutiny of either logic or common
sense. An objective observer might ask, "How do you help
the poor by hurting the rich?" or "How do you help the
jobless by hurting the entrepreneurs who create jobs?" In
truth, the best way to help someone is to empower him to
help himself. America's 26th President, Teddy Roosevelt,
was the personification of the work ethic that helped make
America great. He summarized his thoughts on government sponsored programs that undermine the work ethic

when he said: "[T]he only permanently beneficial way in which to help anyone is to help him help himself; if either private charity, or governmental action, or any form of social expression destroys the individual's power of self-help, the gravest possible wrong is really done the individual."[19]

Socialism does the "gravest possible wrong" (humanly speaking) to the individual because it undermines the character traits most likely to ensure a productive life that contributes to the betterment of society. Arrogantly undermining the character of America is precisely what President Obama and his supporters are doing, and will continue to do, until Americans finally say "enough is enough" and take their country back from those bent on destroying it. Sarah Palin can lead the charge in taking America back by rejecting socialism and committing to the restoration of capitalism, the free market, entrepreneurship, and the traditional work ethic.

President Obama's Broken Promise of No Lobbyists

A characteristic that concerns many Americans—even some who supported his election—is Barack Obama's now obvious propensity for promising one thing but doing another. To many it appears that during the campaign he was willing to say anything to get elected, but now that he is president, Barack Obama either conveniently forgets or arrogantly ignores his promises. For example, consider candidate Obama's promise about keeping lobbyists out of his administration if elected. He made this promise numerous times during his campaign against Senator

John McCain and actually put it in writing on his website (Change.gov):

> I am in this race to tell the corporate lob-
> byists that their days of setting the agenda
> in Washington are over. I have done more
> than any other candidate in this race to
> take on lobbyists—and won. They have not
> funded my campaign, they will not run my
> White House, and they will not drown out
> the voices of the American people.[20]

In her book, *Culture of Corruption,* Michelle Malkin has this to say about how well President Obama has kept this campaign promise: "A year later, he threw open his transition office and the Oval Office to the nation's leading lobbyists and influence peddlers... In the first two weeks of his infant administration... Obama had made seventeen exceptions to his no-lobbyist rule."[21] As examples, Malkin lists the following individuals: Tom Daschle, Eric Holder, Tom Vilsack, Ron Klain, Leon Panetta, Patrick Gaspard, David Hayes, William Corr, and Mark Patterson.[22]

This list is not comprehensive, nor was it intended to be. In fact, the list was growing daily as Malkin wrote her book. A closer look at just one of these individuals shows how blatantly President Obama violated his own injunction against lobbyists. Eric Holder is the 82nd Attorney General of the United States, the first African-American to serve in this position, and a high-level lobbyist at the firm of Covington & Burling from 2001 to 2004. As a lobbyist, his clients included pharmaceutical giant, Merck, the National Football League, Chiquita Brands International, and then Illinois Governor Rod Blagojevich.

Politifact.com maintains a "Truth-O-Meter" on which it tracks 513 campaign promises made by Barack Obama (the type of thing the press and media would be doing if the President happened to be a conservative). According to Politifact.com, during the presidential campaign, Barack Obama claimed numerous times that lobbyists would not be allowed to run his administration or to work on regulations or contracts that related to their former employment as lobbyists for a period of two years. The Obama campaign "delighted in tweaking rival John McCain for the former lobbyists who worked on McCain's campaign."[23] Sarah Palin should be prepared to point out that not only does this president arrogantly break his promises, he can be blatantly hypocritical.

On his first full day in office, President Obama made a big show of signing an executive order supposedly ensuring that any lobbyists hired in his administration would not be allowed to work on projects related to their past employment for a period of two years. But as the American public is fast coming to realize, the President is a master of prevarication and obfuscation. Without calling the attention of the American public to it, President Obama built a convenient loophole into his executive order that allowed for "waivers." This is why Angie Drobnic Holan says that for the Obama administration hiring lobbyists is "...okay if they say it's okay."[24] As we have already learned from Michelle Malkin, Barack Obama jumped through the loophole in his own executive order seventeen times in the first two weeks of his administration.[25] Inconsistencies such as these are grist for the campaign mill for Sarah Palin.

In other words, the executive order President Obama signed restricting the activities of former lobbyists in his administration is nothing but eyewash—an unenforceable public-relations scheme sold to the American public with the willing assistance of this president's favorite public-relations firm—the mainstream media. Rather than just admit the obvious—that he said whatever he had to in order to get elected and never intended to keep his promises—President Obama uses his gift for words to generate a cloud of fog around this issue, as well as others.

After months of cavalierly ignoring his promises, President Obama finally began to generate some pushback. In the summer of 2009, Senator Charles Grassley of Iowa asked the U.S. Office of Government Ethics to require President Obama to provide a full accounting of all waivers and recusals that have been granted to former lobbyists now serving in his administration. Grassley's letter read in part: "The American people deserve a full accounting of all waivers and recusals to better understand who is running the government and whether the administration is adhering to its promise to be open, transparent, and accountable."[26] The American people do indeed deserve a full accounting and Sarah Palin will need to demand one on their behalf.

President Obama's Broken Promise of Transparency

President Obama campaigned on a promise of transparency. His was going to be the most open, honest, and transparent administration in our nation's history. This has not happened. In fact, it is transparency that may be the most prominent of his broken promises. Perhaps the best example of how breaking this promise has affected President Obama came in September 2009 when he decided to speak directly to all school children in America. This decision caused a firestorm of protests from parents nationwide.

The editorial in our local newspaper a few days after President Obama's speech to school children across the country carried the headline, "Much Ado About Nothing." The point the editor tried to make can be paraphrased as follows: "I told you there was nothing to worry about. Why did everyone get so upset about President Obama speaking to school children?" This misguided editor probably spoke for a lot of easily misled Americans who were lulled to sleep by a wily strategist and consummate actor—Barack Obama.

Why all the uproar over a president speaking to school children? This is a legitimate question. After all, those of our generation would have been delighted had President Eisenhower decided to deliver such a speech. The difference, of course, is that President Obama is not President Eisenhower. Eisenhower was trusted by the American people. Even the few who did not "like Ike" trusted him. President Obama, on the other hand, is not trusted by a large and rapidly growing number of Americans because he has broken so many promises.

In our book, *Born to Lie,* we made the point that the most important asset a president can have is the trust of the American people. We showed why President Obama has failed to earn this trust. Public trust is even more important to an American president than a strong military, majority in Congress, or vibrant economy. Without trust, a president will find that his motives are always suspect in the minds of American citizens. Consequently, his actions will always be questioned. Such is the case with President Obama, who has turned out to be one of the most divisive and least trusted presidents ever to occupy the White House. This is the first point that should be understood by the *Much-Ado-About-Nothing* crowd.

The second point that should be understood is this: do not let your guard down. Instead, consider the following issues and remain vigilant:

- Because of the public outcry, the President was forced to reveal the contents of his speech via the Internet beforehand. Had there been no public outcry would this speech have been the one the President gave?

- Because of the public outcry the President was forced to drop his idea of providing lesson plans and curriculum materials to accompany his speech.

- President Obama has now established the precedent of bypassing parents and going directly to their children. These school kids do not understand the issues and are easy prey for an articulate, charismatic speaker. Further, because his first speech was so innocuous and inoffensive, he has lulled many parents to sleep. Once parents are no longer paying attention, what will be the content of future speeches?

- If President Obama continues the practice of speaking directly to school children over what will be at least four years in office, today's tenth graders will have heard him on several occasions by the time they are of voting age. The President has a charismatic personality that young, naive people are likely to find appealing. The President is also smart enough to know that with his speeches he is creating a future voting bloc for himself and his fellow travelers in Congress, based on familiarity and the cult of personality model. The last thing our country needs in these troubled times is young voters casting their ballots to re-elect a president because they think he is "cool."

There is good reason to mistrust President Obama, as he has demonstrated repeatedly since being sworn in. The uproar over his decision to speak directly to school children was hardly much ado about nothing. Rather it was an outgrowth of understandable suspicion on the part of responsible citizens about a president who has failed to earn the trust of the American people because he has repeatedly broken his promise of transparency. Sarah Palin needs to make the point during her campaign that there is something wrong when the American public does not trust its president to speak to school children, and indicates that there is a lack of trust because of the President's deceitful rhetoric and broken promises.

Obama's Broken Promises Concerning the CIA Investigation

During his campaign for the presidency, Barack Obama was asked if he planned to investigate the CIA concerning the techniques it has used when interrogating terrorists. His response was that he planned to "look forward," not back. Then after President Obama had been in office less than a year, his Attorney General, Eric Holder, decided to investigate the CIA for possible abuses committed during interrogations of terrorists. Holder proceeded with his investigation over the vocal objections of President Obama's hand-picked director of the CIA, Leon Panetta, as well as six other former directors of the CIA.

The investigation represents just one more of many broken promises by President Obama. On August 24, 2009, the Obama administration "appointed a special prosecutor to pursue criminal charges against CIA employees who interrogated some of al Qaeda's hardest core members."[27] The fact that Eric Holder is at the center of this controversy represents the perfect irony since he owes his current position to another broken promise by President Obama—the no-lobbyists promise. A further irony and an indication of President Obama's values and judgment is that when Eric Holder served in the Clinton White House he recommended pardons for convicted Puerto Rican terrorists who had murdered people with their bombs.

A reality check is in order here. War is the ugliest of human enterprises, and wars of terrorism are the ugliest of wars. Although President Obama has naively proclaimed otherwise, America is engaged in a war on terrorism. Perhaps a better way to view the situation is this: regardless of the President's assertions to the contrary, terrorists are making war on America, and they do not care what they have to do to win. War is like a street fight with knives—if you restrict your defense to the Marquis of Queensbury rules, you are likely to become a casualty. Such restrictions are what the Obama administration wants to impose on the CIA.

To defend ourselves against enemies who are bent on our destruction and who recognize no limits on their own brutality, America must be prepared to occasionally set aside the Marquis of Queensbury rules and fight fire with fire. Americans who find this fact distasteful should remember that every day throughout the world there are brave Americans putting their lives on the line, doing things children should not see so that those very children can sleep safely at night. In order to protect America's security, the CIA and military must sometimes do things that would not meet with the approval of timid people with weak stomachs.

In order to preempt attacks against America—whether conventional, nuclear, or terrorist in nature—the commander-in-chief and our military personnel need accurate, up-to-date information. One of the principal agencies charged with responsibility for securing, collecting, and analyzing that information is the Central Intelligence Agency (CIA). The CIA was established by the National Security Act of 1947. It is authorized to use a variety of techniques to secure the information needed to keep America safe from its enemies. One of the problems the CIA has always had when dealing with left-leaning politicians is that its biggest victories are when nothing happens. Because of the need for secrecy, the CIA cannot broadcast its many victories in stopping attacks on America before they could occur. The very people who are quick to question the CIA—people like Eric Holder—may be alive today because of what some brave CIA agent did.

At the same time that the Obama/Holder investigation was initiated, the CIA declassified and released documents titled "Khalid Sheikh Mohammad: Preeminent Source On Al Qaeda" and "Detainee Reporting Pivotal for the War Against Al Qaeda." These documents revealed that interrogated terrorists had revealed information that could be invaluable in preventing future attacks and in capturing those who had perpetrated previous attacks. Information in these reports includes: 1) identities of key al Qaeda personnel in a program to develop anthrax attacks against the United States, 2) identities of people al Qaeda had pegged as being suitable for using in attacks on the West, 3) identities of those who made the bomb used to attack the United States Consulate in Karachi, Pakistan in June 2002, and 4) information concerning a plot to attack Camp Lemonier, an American military base in Djibouti, East Africa.[28]

Make no mistake about it, America is engaged in a war on terrorism and no amount of dissembling on the part of President Obama can change that fact. Al Qaeda did not suddenly stop despising America just because Barack Obama was elected. In fact, they probably saw the election as both a welcome relief and an opportunity to plan future attacks. The best friend al Qaeda could have is an American president bent on punishing and shackling the very agency responsible for preempting its ruthless attacks. Apparently, President Obama's idea of fighting terrorists is to circle the wagons and shoot his own people. The fact that he would allow Attorney General Holder to proceed with such an ill-advised investigation raises a hard question: Is President Obama willing to sacrifice American lives to curry favor with the Muslim world? This is a question that Sarah Palin must ask during the next presidential campaign.

Holding President Obama accountable for his actions will be an important strategy for Sarah Palin in the next presidential election. The president is a well-seasoned professional in the art of political prevarication and he has the assistance of the press and media. However, his determination to transform America into a European-style socialist state is beyond question and well-documented. Further, his broken promises are legion and still accumulating. President Obama's economic policies would make him an excellent President of France, but America is not France. His practice of promising one thing but doing another may be politically expedient, but it has not stood him in good stead with Americans who want to be able to trust their president. His dedication to socialism and to transforming America into a socialist state makes it clear that President Obama does not have America's best interests at heart, and that his views and values are at odds with the majority of Americans. Sarah Palin's values stand in sharp contrast to those of President Obama.

Sarah Palin's commitment to capitalism, the free market, entrepreneurship, and the traditional work ethic will appeal to millions of Americans who are concerned about the United States becoming a second-rate socialist state. Her straight-forward honesty, integrity, and trustworthiness will appeal to millions of Americans who believe that no matter how articulately or how glibly it has been done, they have been systematically lied to by President Obama.

NOTES

1. James Delingpole, *Welcome to Obamaland: I Have Seen Your Future and It Doesn't Work* (Washington, DC: Regnery, 2009), 2.

2. *Ibid*, 3.

3. *Ibid.*

4. *Ibid.*

5. Robert Heilbroner, "Socialism," Library of Economics and Liberty. Retrieved from http://www.econlib.org/libary/Enc/Socialism.html on March 26, 2009.

6. *Ibid.*

7. *Ibid.*

8. *Ibid.*

9. D. Elton Trueblood. Retrieved from http://www.waynet.org/people/biography/trueblood.htm on August 8, 2009.

10. Quoted in Alan O. Ebenstein, *Friedrich Hayek: A Biography* (Chicago, IL: University of Chicago Press, 2003), 137.

11. Niall Ferguson, "The World: Why America Outpaces Europe," *The New York Times.* Retrieved from http://query.nytimes.com/gst/fullpage.html?res=9D04E3D91739F93BA35755C0A9659C8 on December 12, 2008.

12. Mark R. Levin, As quoted in Eli Lake, "Levin's *Manifesto* declares war on the statists," *Washington Times*, March 30, 2009, 26.

13. *Ibid.*

14. James Delingpole, 43.

15. David Limbaugh, "Beltway arrogance and blind faith," *Washington Times*, March 30, 2009, 37.

16. *Ibid.*

17. *Ibid.*

18. *Ibid.*

19. President Theodore Roosevelt as quoted in "He's no Teddy Roosevelt," by Marvin Olasky, *World Magazine*, April 11, 2009.

20. Barack Obama, *Change.gov*, *Agenda Ethics Page.* Retrieved from http://change.gove/agenda/ethics_agenda on May 1, 2009.

21. Michelle Malkin, *Culture of Corruption* (Washington, DC: Regnery, 2009), 10-11.

22. *Ibid.*

23. Angie Drobnic Holan, "Former lobbyist in the White House? It's okay if they say it's okay." Retrieved from http://politifact.com/truth-o-meter/promises/promise/240/tougher-rules-against-revolving-door-for-lobbyists-and-former-officials on August 20, 2009.

24. *Ibid.*

25. Malkin, 11.

26. Angie Drobnic Holan, "Grassley demands waivers and recusals on former lobbyists in the Obama administration." Retrieved from http://politifact.com/truth-o-meter/promises/promise/240/tougher-rules-against-revolving-door-for-lobbyists-and-former-officials on August 20.

27. Ben Conery, "CIA interrogators got results, could face charges," *Washington Times*, August 31, 2009, 18.

28. *Ibid.*

Seven

PRACTICAL ACTIVISM

With its red state/blue state makeup, America's population is now split almost evenly between the left and the right. Consequently, it is independent voters—those in the middle of the political spectrum—that typically swing a presidential election one way or the other. Presidential candidates now win by holding their base of support on either the right or the left and appealing to a majority of those in the middle. It is the rare candidate that can actually pull voters away from the opposing party. The last presidential candidate to do this was Ronald Reagan.

In fact, Reagan's appeal was so strong that many Democrats not only crossed over and voted for him, they left their party and became Republicans. Thus was born the Republican Revolution led by Ronald Reagan. These former Democrats explained their change of party by saying, "We didn't leave the Democrat Party—it left us." By this they meant that their old party had veered too far to the left. Of course, even Reagan's most ardent admirers admit that the Republican Revolution got a lot of help from Jimmy Carter.

By veering even farther to the left, President Obama is setting the stage for another Reagan-like revolution—this one drawing more from the ranks of the independents than from Democrats. The lines between Democrats and

Republicans are more firmly drawn now than they were during the Reagan era. In fact, one of the most significant contemporary political trends is the rise of the independent voter. Rather than move from one party to the other, today's disenchanted voter is more likely to become an independent. Party loyalty is much less a factor today than it was in times past. Independent voters select the candidate who appeals to them most strongly on a personal level. This is good news for Sarah Palin because she has broad personal appeal to the same voters who elected Ronald Reagan.

President Obama's socialist domestic agenda, weak foreign policy, and broken campaign promises are doing for Sarah Palin what Jimmy Carter's botched handling of the Iran hostage crisis and the Middle-East oil embargo did for Ronald Reagan. When he ran against Carter, Ronald Reagan was able to ask the American public a simple question that resounded all the way to the ballot box: "Are you better off today than you were four years ago?" Few people were. Those who weren't answered Reagan's question with their votes.

Independents voted for Barack Obama for a variety of reasons. Some were unhappy with the war in Iraq, some were upset about the budget deficit and burgeoning federal debt, some were concerned about the state of the economy, and some were simply interested in seeing an African-American elected president. In addition, John McCain failed to do what every presidential candidate must do in these days of hard lines between the right and the left— hold his base. The right wing of the Republican Party never warmed to John McCain. Consequently, some of them expressed their dissatisfaction by voting for various third-party candidates while others simply stayed home and did not vote.

Naming Sarah Palin as his running mate gave John McCain a brief ray of hope, but two factors came together to negate the potential she brought to his ailing campaign. First, McCain's advisors made the monumental mistake of putting a muzzle and a leash on Sarah Palin, trying to re-mold her in their tepid image. By doing so they neutralized the value she brought to the ticket. Second, they forgot one of the most fundamental rules of presidential politics: the top of the ticket wins or loses the election no matter how appealing the bottom of the ticket may be.

From Main Street to Pennsylvania Avenue

In order to successfully make the trip from Wasilla to Washington, Sarah Palin will need to run a Reagan-like campaign that appeals to everyday Americans on a personal level. By this we mean a campaign that honors what it means to be an American, restores America's pride and patriotism, advocates capitalism and free-market economics, supports the military, stands up to our enemies throughout the world, and promotes such traditional American values as thrift, diligence, responsibility, accountability, deferred gratification, and hard work. We also mean hanging Barack Obama's record around his neck like a political albatross.

In this book we have proposed six broad strategies that, if implemented effectively, will allow Sarah Palin to defeat Barack Obama in the same way that Ronald Reagan defeated Jimmy Carter. These six strategies are worth reviewing.

- *Be Sarah Palin—refuse to be leashed, muzzled, or remolded by timid advisors.*

- *Commit to restoring the sovereignty and integrity of the Constitution.*

- *Reject socialism—commit to restoring capitalism, entrepreneurship, and the traditional work ethic.* Sarah Palin exemplifies America's entrepreneurial spirit and traditional work ethic. This will be important in the next presidential election. After four years of President Obama's socialist economic policies in the form of bailouts, handouts, and entitlements, America will be ready for a leader who is committed to restoring the entrepreneurial spirit and traditional work ethic.

- *Be forthright in pointing out the failings of secular humanism and unapologetic about America's Christian heritage.* President Obama's absurd denials of America's Christian heritage have made many Americans uncomfortable. More than 70 percent of Americans claim to be Christians. Consequently, after four years of being snubbed by President Obama, Americans will be ready for a candidate who is forthright about the failings of secular humanism and unapologetic about our country's Christian heritage.

- *Do not apologize to our allies or enemies—put America first in foreign policy and support the military.* Many Americans were shocked and even angered when shortly after being elected President Obama went on what came to be known as his *worldwide apology tour.* These same Americans became concerned when President Obama appeared to be timid and ineffective in the conduct of foreign policy. After four years of dangerous weakness in foreign affairs, America will be ready for a strong leader who is a cross between Ronald Reagan and Teddy Roosevelt in foreign policy and who supports the military.

• *Hold Barack Obama responsible for his socialist policies and broken promises.* Many Americans, including some who supported him, are concerned that President Obama is determined to transform the United States into a European-style socialist state. His economic and social policies are so antithetical to Americans that many now question if the President is even an American at heart. Further, many Americans are unable to trust President Obama because he has broken so many of his campaign promises. After four years of socialism and broken promises, Americans will be ready for a president who believes in capitalism and who can be trusted to keep promises.

These six strategies represent the basics of what we believe Sarah Palin must do in order to motivate those on the right while simultaneously pulling in a majority of independents, as well as some moderate Democrats who are disgusted with President Obama's extreme left-wing policies and actions. We do not mean to imply that these six strategies are all that Sarah Palin will have to do. Rather, they are the building blocks that will provide a solid foundation for a winning campaign. Of the various other things that need to be done, three stand out: 1) pulling a "Harry Truman" on traditional press and media outlets by going directly to the American people, 2) committing to making America energy independent, and 3) applying the "dogcatcher principle."

Pulling a "Harry Truman"

Sarah Palin can expect no help from the mainstream press and media in the next presidential election. In fact, she can expect just the opposite. The pro-left bias displayed by the press and media during Barack Obama's campaign and first term in office will be even worse—if that is possible—in the next election. This is because liberal pundits will sense the vulnerability of their favorite son and act accordingly. Consequently, Sarah Palin will need to pull a "Harry Truman" on the mainstream media and take her message directly to the American people.

Students of presidential elections are familiar with the famous photograph of the victorious President Truman holding up a copy of the *Chicago Tribune* which carries a banner headline proclaiming: "Dewey Defeats Truman." Convinced that Thomas Dewey would trounce Truman, the *Trib* prematurely printed an inaccurate result. While Dewey and his advisors blithely put their trust in the supposed wisdom of newspapers opinion polls, Harry Truman busily crisscrossed the country speaking directly to Americans from the back of a train. His strategy of going around the press paid off. Harry Truman won an election that even his supporters thought he would lose.

Although the vehicle used in the next election will be different, the concept will be the same. Like Truman, Sarah Palin will need to go around the press and media and take her case directly to the American people. Fortunately, she has a head start. As soon as Sarah Palin stepped down as Governor of Alaska, she began using the Internet, especially Facebook, as her vehicle for staying in touch with the American people. The strategy is already working. Relying almost exclusively on social networking, Sarah Palin has made her voice and views heard on the various major issues that interest the American public.

In August 2009, when she used Facebook to say that the end-of-life component in their proposed healthcare bill created "death panels," the resulting public outcry forced President Obama and the Democrat-controlled Congress to scrap this irksome provision of the bill. While most political candidates now use the Internet as a campaign tool, Sarah Palin has enjoyed more success with it than most. Political strategist Mary Matalin attributes Sarah Palin's effectiveness on Facebook to empathy on the part of Americans who know she has been unfairly treated by the mainstream press and media.[1]

We agree that the empathy factor is part of the reason for Palin's successful social networking, but think there is more to it than that. Social networking is an effective tool for Sarah Palin because she appeals to everyday Americans on a personal level. They are comfortable with her and relate to her as someone they would like to sit down and have a conversation with. Consequently, Americans want to network with her. As we explained in the first chapter of this book, one of Sarah's greatest strengths is her girl-next-door appeal that makes grassroots Americans feel as if they know her. Even without the assistance of the press and media and the constant exposure that comes with being president, Sarah Palin still has more Facebook "friends" than anyone else on the site other than President Obama.[2]

Facebook might be even more effective for Sarah Palin than other candidates because the press and media, jolted by her sudden popularity, tried hard to paint her as an uninformed upstart who was incapable of handling the tough issues of the presidency. Facebook allows Sarah Palin to refute this ridiculous assertion by showing in print that she is not only conversant with the issues, but well-informed and articulate when stating opinions about them. Whereas the mainstream media will edit her interviews and speeches in ways that serve their own purposes, on Facebook Sarah Palin can go into as much depth as she wants on an issue without fear of interference by journalists pushing a left-wing agenda.

In the interim between now and the next presidential campaign, Sarah Palin has an opportunity to fill in gaps in her experience as appropriate and keep her supporters up to date using her obvious talent for social networking. According to former White House press secretary, Ari

Fleischer, Sarah Palin "represents a gigantic movement in this country that is distrustful of Washington and finds her appealing for all the same reasons that the mainstream media finds her unappealing. This is where social networks are most effective. [They] let you focus on your core constituents and fan base, and few politicians can actually claim they have a fan base."[3]

Committing to Energy Independence

"A powerful idea is spreading through America. It is a call to this generation to take action and decide the course of history by declaring and fighting for American Energy Independence."[4] Oil is America's economic Achilles heel. It affects America's national security, economy, and the environment. As such, oil colors the thinking of America's leaders in all aspects of domestic and foreign policy. Oil allows rogue nations with unpredictable leaders who hate the United States to dictate terms in the global game of geopolitical hegemony. Oil gives otherwise inconsequential nations immense leverage in determining the balance of power worldwide. This situation cannot be allowed to persist.

No candidate in the next election will be able to match Sarah Palin's hands-on experience in dealing with energy issues. She has served as Governor of the most important state in the nation when it comes to energy. She has gone eye-to-eye with stubborn oil executives and stared them down. Consequently, she has the experience and credibility to lead America in making a firm commitment to energy independence.

To grasp just how dependent the United States has become on foreign oil, consider the following facts:

- American drivers consume approximately 378 million gallons of gasoline (about nine million barrels of oil). This is 45 percent of total oil consumption in the United States.

- America consumes 20 million barrels of oil products daily (nine million of this is for gasoline).

- America imports approximately 10 million barrels of crude oil daily, six million of which come from OPEC countries.[5]

> Today, over 80 percent of world petroleum reserves are state-owned—controlled by countries that have the power to manipulate supply and price with impunity—this fact goes directly to the heart of energy security. The phrase *'Energy Independence'* is a slogan embodying an idea that resonates with the character of America—it is a call for return to economic balance and protection from vulnerability created by overdependence on petroleum to fuel our cars, trucks, and airplanes—it is a public outcry voiced by citizens demanding government leadership in energy production, distribution, and fuel choice.[6]

This is not a message meant to get government involved in the production and distribution of oil, but rather a call for government leadership that will empower the private sector and individual Americans to do their part in establishing energy independence. Government leadership will have to begin at the top with the President of the United States. That leadership is not being provided by Barack Obama. Sarah Palin can be the one who finally makes Americans aware of what needs to be done to achieve energy independence and who can also lead them in getting it done.

The Dogcatcher Principle

The final strategy that must be employed is what has been referred to as the "dogcatcher principle." Failure to apply this principle is one of the main reasons that third-parties never gain any traction in presidential elections. The dogcatcher principle posits that the way for a political party to effect change is to begin at the local level—by electing "dogcatchers." The concept of the dogcatcher includes all local political offices: city council, county commission, school board, tax collector, property appraiser, and judges. Democrat Speaker of the House, Tip O'Neill, was paraphrasing the dogcatcher principle when he asserted that "all politics is local."

Applying the dogcatcher principle involves building grassroots support—starting at the bottom rather than the top. This is why third-party candidates do so poorly in presidential elections—they insist on starting at the top. Third parties tend to run for one office and one office only: president. But change begins at the grassroots level; it is a bottom-up not a top-down enterprise. Sarah Palin got where she is today by first getting involved in the PTA. She didn't set out to be President of the United States, but her successful track record of local concern and activism opened door after door of opportunity. Her example of utilizing the dogcatcher principle should encourage conservatives across America to win seats on city councils, county commissions, and school boards. This does not mean that we ignore Republicans seeking state and federal offices. On the contrary, it means that conservatives should be seeking office at *every* level of government.

Sarah Palin is ideally suited to promote the dogcatcher principle because she has used it successfully in her own career. When she ran for Mayor of Wasilla, she was applying the dogcatcher principle. Winning this grassroots position helped catapult her to the governorship of Alaska which, in turn, helped make her a viable candidate for the presidency. The dogcatcher principle is especially important in Sarah Palin's case because the mainstream media will do everything in its considerable power to undermine her candidacy. However, their biased reporting will fall on deaf ears at the grassroots level when local office holders owe their success to her "dogcatcher" example. In fact, if the "Harry Truman" strategy is used effectively, the contrary efforts of the mainstream media could very well backfire on them.

Applying the dogcatcher principle would seem to be the commonsense approach of any political candidate, but surprisingly it is not. Paul Weyrich—a man who knows how to get people elected—once lamented the fact that he could get all the candidates he wanted if he offered to fund their campaign for the United States Senate, but not for lower offices. In fact, the lower the office the more reluctant candidates are to step forward and run. This reluctance is a golden opportunity for conservatives to step up and fill these lower offices, providing the grass-roots level support that will be critical if the Republican Party is going to prevail in 2012. Sarah Palin has the experience and is perfectly suited to lead this national rebuilding project.

Conclusion

Within minutes of the announcement that Barack Obama had been elected President, media pundits were telling the world that Sarah Plain had no chance of winning the Republican nomination for President in 2012. Although this is probably just wishful thinking on the part of left-leaning journalists, it does raise an interesting question. With the economy struggling, unemployment at record levels, two wars being fought in foreign lands, rogue nations developing nuclear weapons, and an ever-growing energy dependence on countries that hate America, will Sarah Palin even want the job? No one could blame her if she said "no."

On the other hand, the fact that a biased mainstream media is already doing its best to undermine her candidacy reveals an interesting fact: Sarah Palin has become the leading spokesperson for the Republican Party. No other likely Republican candidate concerns Democrats or their friends in the mainstream media as much as Sarah. She is the one conservative voice that Americans across the board will listen to.

The Republicans now face the same problem that

haunted the Democrats in 1968: no official spokesperson for the party. Lyndon Johnson had made his famous televised address in which he informed the nation he would neither seek nor accept his party's nomination for president.   Hubert Humphrey was not a viable spokesperson for the Democrats because he had just lost the 1968 election to Richard Nixon. The unwritten rules of presidential politics had changed since 1952. In 1952, Adlai Stevenson had been defeated by Eisenhower, yet he was still the Democratic front-runner and spokesperson in 1956. The same was true of Tom Dewey after his defeat in 1944. Presidential candidates could get another chance back then. Nixon was able to get two additional chances after losing to John F. Kennedy in 1960, then to Pat Brown in California's gubernatorial race in 1962. In spite of these defeats, Nixon was able to stage a comeback and win the Republican nomination as well as the presidency. However, after 1968 things changed in presidential politics. The unwritten rule became "you get one shot and one shot only."

In 1961, after Nixon's loss, the titular head of the Republican Party was Dwight D. Eisenhower. He had served two full terms and was the Grand Old Man of the Grand Old Party. As a former President, he was expected by informal protocol to say nothing negative—at least in public—about President Kennedy's policies or performance. However, he could give unofficial advice to those who visited his Gettysburg home, and many did. In his retirement, George W. Bush's situation is more like Lyndon Johnson's than Eisenhower's. He left office while a war still raged—always a

negative for a president—and while the economy was col-
lapsing—an even greater negative. Consequently, he cannot be the spokesperson for the Republican Party nor can
he openly criticize Barack Obama. Under the post-1968
rules of Presidential politics, John McCain has become the
equivalent of Hubert Humphrey in 1969, George McGov-
ern in 1973, and Walter Mondale in 1985. He can return to
the Senate and eventually retire gracefully, but he cannot
be the spokesperson for his party.

Most modern presidents have followed four paths to the
Presidency: Vice President, the Senate, a governorship, or a
successful generalship in a popular major war. Following
Barack Obama's election victory, Republicans have no eligible Vice President to run. Viable Republican candidates
from the Senate are also scarce. With the Democrats in
control of the upper house of Congress, Republican Senators
are struggling—without success—to gain sufficient media
attention to become viable candidates. Republican Senators
are almost invisible—not one of them can claim national
recognition. The only sitting governor who is widely-known
outside of his own state is Arnold Schwarzenegger, and he is
not eligible to run for president. This not only makes Sarah
Palin the unofficial spokesperson for the Republican Party,
it leaves her in the optimum position to win the Republican
nomination. As a Washington outsider, she is also the only
candidate poised to challenge the mindless cycle of beltway
politics as usual. In other words, when it comes to unseating
Barack Obama in 2012, the best man for the job might just
be a woman and that woman is Sarah Palin.

NOTES:

1. "Palin emerges as Facebook phenom." Retrieved from http://news.yahoo.com/s/politico/20090919/pl_politico/27344 on September 20, 2009.

2. *Ibid.*

3. As quoted in "Palin emerges as Facebook phenom." Retrieved from http://news.yahoo.com/s/politico/20090919/pl_politico/27344 on September 20, 2009.

4. American Energy Independence. "Energy Independence." Retrieved from http://www.americanenergyindependence.com on September 23, 2009.

5. *Ibid.*

6. *Ibid.*